Courage is ~~fea~~ The~~i~~

Courage is mastery of fear, not absence
of fear.
Mark Twain

Step Up

Other books by Richard C. Meyer:

One Anothering, Volume 1:
Biblical Building Blocks for Small Groups

One Anothering, Volume 2:
Building Spiritual Community in Small Groups

One Anothering, Volume 3:
Creating Significant Spiritual Community

About the Author

Richard Meyer served the Presbyterian Church USA in pastoral ministry for twenty-five years. In the fall of 2000, he left pastoral ministry and founded The One Anothering Institute, which is committed to training congregations and individuals in making small groups a lifestyle rather than a program in the church.

He is a conference speaker, small group consultant, retreat leader, margin question writer for *Serendipity's Interactive Bible Study,* and a regular columnist for *Faith @ Work Magazine.* His three volume *One Anothering* series, based on the "One Another" passages in the Bible, has been called "the best books for small groups I have ever seen!"

He received his B.A. from UCLA, and his M.Div. and D. Min. from Fuller Theological Seminary in Pasadena, California. He is married to Trudy, and has two adult children and one grandchild.

For additional information on Richard and the One Anothering Institute, go to www.oneanothering.com.

STEP UP

A Vital Process for Spiritual Renewal

Richard C. Meyer

Augsburg Books
MINNEAPOLIS

STEP UP
A Vital Process for Spiritual Renewal

Large-quantity purchases or custom editions of this book are available at a discount from the publisher. For more information, contact the sales department at Augsburg Fortress, Publishers, 1-800-328-4648, or write to: Sales Director, Augsburg Fortress, Publishers, P. O. Box 1209, Minneapolis, MN 55440-1209.

The Twelve Steps are adapted with permission of Alcoholics Anonymous World Services, Inc. (A.A.W.S.) Permission to adapt the Twelve Steps does not mean that A.A.W.S. has reviewed or approved the contents of this publication, or that A.A.W.S. necessarily agrees with the views expressed herein. A.A. is a program of recovery from alcoholism only—use of the Twelve Steps in connection with programs and activities which are patterned after A.A., but which address other problems, or in any other non-A.A. context, does not imply otherwise.

Scripture quotations are from the New Revised Standard Version Bible, copyright © 1989 by the Division of Christian Education of the National Council of the Churches of Christ in the USA. Used by permission.

Library of Congress Cataloging-in-Publication Data
Meyer, Richard C., 1948-
  Step up : a vital process for spiritual renewal / by Richard C. Meyer.
      p. cm.
  Includes bibliographical references.
  ISBN 0-8066-5135-0 (alk. paper)
  1. Spiritual life—Christianity. 2. Twelve-step programs—Religious aspects—Christianity.
I. Title.
  BV4501.3.M496 2005
  248.8'629—dc22   2004026348

Cover design by Dave Meyer; cover art from Getty Images
Book design by Michelle L. N. Cook

The paper used in this publication meets the minimum requirements of American National Standard for Information Sciences—Permanence of Paper for Printed Library Materials, ANSI Z329.48-1984. ♾ ™

Manufactured in the U.S.A.

09   08   07   06   05   1   2   3   4   5   6   7   8   9   10

Thanks:

To my editor, Marcia Broucek,
for her wonderful way with words and perceptive comments.

To my wife, Trudy, and friend Susan Smith,
for hours of proofreading and their encouraging suggestions.

To my "full of grace" Twelve Step friends, Dave Wallace, Ferd Payne,
Steve Foreman, and Marty and Bro Lemen,
whose lives caused me to investigate the Twelve Steps.

To my mother, Betty Cardona,
who loved me through her battle with alcohol as best she could.

To the Faith at Work community
and their commitment to honest and authentic spirituality.

Table of Contents

Introduction

A young boy got off the school bus, said good-bye to his friends, and walked the half block to his home. As he approached the door, the familiar knot in his stomach surfaced. He reached for the door-knob, took a deep breath, and hoped for the best. "Maybe she did not take a drink today," he thought to himself. He hated it when she drank. Under the influence of alcohol, his mother became a different person. Her face changed. Her words became "sugary sweet," but you could not let the "sweetness" fool you. You had to watch your step during this metamor-phosis. Any little misstep on your part could set her off. She possessed a hair-trigger temper when she drank. She would often lash out at a family member, storm off, and slam the bedroom door behind her. Then the next day, it was as if it never happened. No one in the family dared bring it up. They just hoped to get through the next day without another "incident." With his heart pounding, he opened the door and yelled, "Hi, Mom. I'm home." Then he waited. The tone of her voice would tip him off. Would there be hell to pay or would everything be all right?

The above scenario is not fictional. I was that young boy. I was the one on the school bus. I was the one who prepared for the worst on the ride home. I was the one with the knot in his stomach as he reached for the doorknob. As a child, that's how I coped: prepare for the worst so you do not get caught by surprise; anticipate a problem that is next to impossible to solve; expect to get chewed out for doing something wrong. It was like living in a minefield. Who knew when my mother would explode? I am a grandfather now, but that little boy still resides in me. The scars of growing up in an alcoholic family remain. If not careful, I fall into my old childhood patterns of coping with the unknown lurking behind closed doors. I have to work on not expecting the other shoe to drop. I have to concentrate on not immediately imagining worst-case scenarios. I have to battle the urge to keep everyone happy. I'm sure that's why, in part, I married such an optimist. Surely, subconsciously, I expected Trudy's optimism to rub off on me. Certainly, she would teach me how to view the challenges of life more positively. Definitely, she would help me to realize that potential disaster does not lurk behind every door.

I further suspect my going to seminary shortly after college had as much do with justifying my sanity, as it did a sense of call. Something deep inside of me said, "See, Mom, it wasn't me, it was you. I'm a good boy. I've gone to seminary. Do you see now that you were wrong about me? Do you see now that all those mean things you said about me before you stormed off and shut yourself in your room were not true?" My younger sister eventually moved out of the house at age twelve. She could not handle the lunacy any more. She lived the remainder of her adolescent years with our father, who had divorced my mother when I was six and my sister was less than a year old. He could not take the madness either. My mother remarried when I was twelve. My stepfather, Nick, died of a stroke at the age of fifty-one. I suspect it had something to do with the strain of living with an alcoholic spouse. Nick did his best to become a buffer for my sister and me. When my mother "went off" and stormed out of the room, he assured us it was her and not us. Those words helped, but not enough. Later, I would learn he was a classic "enabler." He cleaned up her messes rather than confronted the root of the problem.

After seminary, my wife and I moved to our first church in Omaha, Nebraska. Our friends thought we were nuts. Why go to Omaha, Nebraska? Why not stay in California? Who would want to live in Omaha? We soon discovered what God had in mind for us. After moving, we met some practitioners of the Twelve Steps of Alcoholics Anonymous. Some involved themselves in AA, some Al-Anon, and some as Adult Children of Alcoholics. I found these people deeply spiritual, wonderfully relational, and transparently honest. In fact, their transparency rubbed off on others. As they openly shared their faith journeys and their stories of recovery, they freed others in the congregation to share their needs, struggles, and experiences of God. They also seemed to be maturing in the faith at a faster pace than the rest of us. What did they know that the rest of us did not?

I discovered that they possessed a time-tested, working model for transformation, not just spiritual transformation, but emotional and relational transformation as well. As I listened to them describe the different "Steps" in the model, I realized how each Step has roots in Scripture. Although the Steps might not use "churchy" or "religious" language, they are each biblically sound. Think of them as the "Cliff Notes" version of the Bible or the shorthand version of the faith:

Step One touches on the human condition of being powerless over sin.
Step Two touches on faith and trust.
Step Three touches on surrender.
Steps Four and Five touch on confession.
Steps Six through Nine touch on repentance.
Steps Ten through Twelve touch upon ongoing spiritual renewal.

Since meeting these folks in Nebraska, I've used the Steps regularly and beneficially in my own spiritual journey. I know you will find them helpful as well. As you work through this book, I encourage you to do so with a trusted friend or a group of friends. I have included sharing and reflection questions at the end of each chapter to share with one another. If you do this as a small group, let me recommend some group practices.

First, what's shared in the group stays in the group. Confidentiality in a small group is essential. We need to know that other group members will treat our sharing as a sacred trust. If we cannot depend on each other to keep confidences, we will be reluctant to share our doubts, fears, joys, hopes, and needs. The success of the Steps requires radical honesty.

Second, the group leader answers each sharing question first. The leader needs to be willing to share at the level he or she expects others to share. Called "modeling," sharing first gives group members time to process their responses to the question, as well as an idea of how long and how deeply to share. Generally speaking, people will not share more deeply than the group leader. "Modeling" sets the tone for the sharing level of the group.

Third, people have permission to pass. Participants need to know that they will not be asked to share anything they are not ready to share. While we hope all will take part fully in the group experience, sometimes a question may seem too personal or threatening. If asked to share too much, group members may be unwilling to come back for future meetings. Giving people permission to pass assures group members that this will be a safe place and that their personal boundaries will be honored.

Fourth, the group begins and ends on time. Some become resentful if they have worked hard to get to a meeting only to have the meeting delayed because others arrived late. I know I do. Others need to be at work or pick up a baby-sitter shortly after the meeting and need the group to end promptly. By beginning and ending punctually, we respect each other's time. If some desire more social time together, they always have the freedom to come early or stay after the meeting.

In a television interview, singer Celine Dion made an astute comment. Reflecting on the line from the Barbra Streisand hit song "People," Dion said, "One would have expected the line to read, 'People, who *do not* need people are the luckiest people in the world.' Dion thought for a moment and said, "Of course, 'needing people' makes sense. When you are vulnerable and open yourself up to others, you have an opportunity to receive more love."

I hope that is your experience with this book. As you open yourself to God and others, I hope you will experience a good measure of grace, forgiveness, peace, and love.

Section One

The Give Up Steps

"I give up trying to reason with you."

"I give up. I'll never balance the checkbook."

"I have looked everywhere for those sunglasses. I give up. They must be gone."

"I give up. I will never understand you!"

"I'll never be able to do this. I give up."

"We've given up trying to make sense of this."

Songwriter and singer Neil Sedaka told us that "breaking up is hard to do," but so is "giving up." "Giving up" is often dreadfully difficult and deeply frustrating. We would rather "hang in there" or "give it our best shot" or "persevere to the end" than "give up." "Giving up" reminds us of our limitations and our need for help. "Giving up" reminds us that we are not all powerful. "Giving up" is hard to do.

I think of a friend who asked me what I was writing. I told him, "I'm writing a book about the theological and biblical foundation of the Twelve Steps." He said, "Those Twelve Steps are tough. I've never gotten beyond the First Step, and I've been working on that Step my entire life!"

"Giving up" is difficult, and we might not welcome this first group of Steps, yet they are at the very core of spiritual renewal. They enable us to see ourselves for who we are and to trust the One who can ultimately heal our souls. These first three Steps ask us to admit we cannot fix ourselves and to surrender to the One who can. Step One defines the problem. Step Two provides the cure. Step Three outlines the condition we must meet to activate the cure.

Step One: We admitted we were powerless over [sin]—that our lives had become unmanageable.

Step Two: We came to believe that a Power greater than ourselves could restore us to sanity.

Step Three: We made a decision to turn our wills and our lives over to the care of God *as we understood [God].*

Chapter 1

The Great Admission

Step One: We admitted we were powerless over [sin]—that our lives had become unmanageable.

On her tiptoes Marty stands no more than five-feet-two-inches tall. She has radiant, snow-white hair. She loves bird watching, hiking, native flora and fauna. She taught my son to fish and snapped a picture of his first catch. She has a great recipe for pork tenderloin, and it's one of our family's favorite meals. Whenever we have it, we appropriately dub it our "Marty Meal." Marty and her husband, Bro, have been married for fifty-plus years. They have not all been easy, especially after Bro's stroke, and before that, when Bro had been drinking. Marty served as lay coordinator of our small group ministry in our congregation in Omaha. She also regularly attended Al-Anon meetings. Based on the Twelve Steps, Al-Anon offers understanding help and support to families and friends of problem drinkers. One evening Marty leaned over to me and said, "As I look back on all those years attending Al-Anon, I realize that often those groups acted more like the church than the church. The majority of the people I met there were much more authentic and grace-filled than those I met in the church."

Author Philip Yancey shares something similar in his book *What's So Amazing About Grace?* He reflects on the Alcoholic Anonymous group that meets in the basement of his church and says:

> I sometimes attended AA as an act of solidarity with a recovering alcoholic friend. The first time I accompanied him I was overwhelmed by what I found, for in many ways it resembled the New Testament church. A well-known television broadcaster and several prominent millionaires mixed freely with unemployed dropouts and kids who wore Band-Aids to hide the needle marks on their arms. The "sharing time" was like a textbook small group, marked by compassionate listening, warm responses, and many hugs. Introductions went like this: "Hi, I'm Tom, and I'm an alcoholic." Instantly everyone shouted in unison, like a Greek chorus, "Hi, Tom."
>
> Sometimes as I went up and down the stairs connecting our church sanctuary to the basement, I thought of the upstairs/downstairs contrast between Sunday mornings and Tuesday evenings. Only a few of those who met on Tuesday evenings returned on Sundays. Though they appreciated the church's generosity in opening its basement to them, the AA members I talked with said they would not feel at ease in church. Upstairs people seemed to have it together, while they were just barely hanging on. They felt more comfortable in the swirl of blue smoke, slouched in metal chairs in jeans and a T-shirt.
>
> If only they realized, if only the church could realize, that in some of the most important lessons of spirituality, members of the basement group were our masters. They began with radical honesty and ended with radical dependence.[1]

A friend and practitioner of the Twelve Steps calls the writing of the Steps the greatest event of the past century. I might rank a number of other twentieth-century events ahead of the founding of Alcoholics Anonymous (such as the two World Wars, the discovery of the polio vaccine, the beginning of the space age, and the advent of computers), but I would certainly place AA and the Twelve Steps in the top ten. The Steps provide a model of spiritual healing and growth that has not only spread like wildfire over the past few decades, but also has provided a useful and potent model of spiritual healing and growth. They are for anyone who wants to live a full and meaningful life, not just alcoholics.

A Brief History

The Twelve Steps grew out of the Oxford Group, an early small group movement committed to eight spiritual disciplines: surrender; sharing; restitution; quiet time; guidance; witness; fellowship; and the four absolutes—absolute love, absolute honesty, absolute unselfishness, and absolute purity. Originally called a "First Century Christian Fellowship," this evangelical movement aimed to bring spiritual renewal into the lives of individuals. The Oxford Group also had a good track record in working with alcoholics. One such person was Ebby Thatcher.

In the early 1930s Ebby began attending Oxford Group meetings at the Calvary Episcopal Church in New York City. After applying the Oxford Group's principles and practices, he realized he was no longer battling alcohol. He felt liberated from it. Excited about his experience, he invited his friend Bill Wilson, a stockbroker on Wall Street and fellow alcoholic, to one of the Oxford meetings. Eventually, Bill Wilson also had a significant experience of God, as well as release from his drinking, through Calvary Church and the Oxford movement.

Later Bill W. traveled to Akron, Ohio, on business. Shortly after arriving, he desperately desired a drink. Realizing his dangerous state of mind, he looked for an Oxford Group meeting in Akron. He found one, and while there met his polar opposite, Dr. Bob Smith. Dr. Bob was stern, distant, and a silent drinker. Bill W. was a self-important, boisterous New York City alcoholic. Despite differing personalities, they became fast friends. Bill W. stayed at Dr. Bob's house for months. They went to regular Oxford meetings together, inviting their alcoholic friends to join them. On June 10, 1935, in Akron, Dr. Bob took his last drink and became one of the co-founders of Alcoholics Anonymous. A few years later, both New York and Akron alcoholics split from the Oxford movement because the group was too religious and too preachy for other alcoholics.

The Oxford movement, however, left its mark. Influenced by the principles of the movement, the teaching of Rev. Sam Shoemaker at Calvary Episcopal Church, and late night discussions with Dr. Bob, Bill W. took what he had learned and experienced and wrote the Twelve Steps in December of 1938. After running the Steps by other alcoholics, Bill W. published the "Big Book" of AA in 1939, appropriately titled *Alcoholics Anonymous.* Bill Wilson said,

> It was from Sam that co-founder Dr. Bob and I in the beginning absorbed most of the principles that were afterward embodied in the Twelve Steps of Alcoholics Anonymous, steps that express the heart of AA's way of life. Dr. Silkworth gave us the needed knowledge of our illness, but Sam Shoemaker gave us the concrete knowledge of what we could do about it. One showed us the mysteries of the lock that held us in prison; the other passed on the spiritual keys by which we are limited.[2]

Sam Shoemaker alluded to the scriptural roots of the Steps at the twentieth anniversary Alcoholics Anonymous convention, saying, "AA derived much of its inspiration from the church. Now perhaps the time has come for the church to be re-awakened and re-vitalized by those insights and practices found in AA."

Some people of faith, however, object to the secular language of the Twelve Steps. In fact, many have dismissed the Steps as unbiblical and unchristian. Using the term "Higher Power," instead of "God" or "Jesus Christ," bothers them. Deciding to turn our lives over to "God as we understand him" sounds like slippery, New Age jargon. In reality, that could not be further from the truth. Bill W. and Dr. Bob, both Christians, knew many drunks would dismiss the Steps if they sounded too religious or churchy. The church, after all, had been very condemning, judgmental, and hurtful toward their alcoholic friends and acquaintances. History has proven them right. The "Higher Power" language has moved great numbers of men and women into an authentic faith in the God of Scripture, and into an intimate relationship with Jesus Christ. Patricia Campbell-Schmitt, Presbyterian pastor and one-time clergy consultant to a Twelve Step treatment center, relates the following experience:

> In those early weeks of my work at the treatment center, one man stands out. I'll call him Stan. Stan was a marine biologist, a brilliant scientist who began his alcoholic drinking twenty-five years earlier following the death of his young wife from a painful, debilitating form of cancer. His wife's death not only left Stan drowning his grief in a bottle, but also left him with no hope of ever believing in a caring, compassionate God. In our first meeting together, Stan admitted that he needed help from something beyond himself, but there was no way he was going to call his Higher Power "God." Instead, he chose to describe his Higher Power as a "Cosmic Force." Two weeks later I met with Stan again. "Patty," he said, "I've discovered that the cosmic force wasn't enough for me. In the last week I've discovered that my Higher Power is a divine being, a loving God who everyday seems more and more like that man from Nazareth."[3]

Others have had similar experiences. Most importantly, the Steps work. There's a great cartoon line that asks, "How do I get to Friday?" While not magic, that is precisely what the Twelve Steps have helped millions of people do: get from Monday to Friday. They have enabled people get to where they want, and need, to go. God has used the Steps to relieve suffering, fill emptiness, and foster emotional, relational, mental, and spiritual renewal. The Steps do not come with a hundred percent money-back guarantee. They are not fun to do. They are even harder to follow. But they offer a vital process for spiritual renewal.

Half of the people in my Wednesday night small group have previously been in Twelve Step groups. As a result, at the end of our group, we use a closing exercise that we borrowed from their Twelve Step groups. We gather in a circle, join hands, say the Lord's Prayer in unison. After the prayer we exclaim together, "Keep coming back, it works!" When put into practice, the Steps work.

In preparing to work through these Steps, keep two things in mind. One, the Twelve Steps are progressive. They build upon one another. We need to work through them systematically and in order. Two, we never finish working on them. We always have "sins" and "issues" that we need to work on throughout our lives. We never "arrive," this side of heaven.

Every journey begins with a first step. Let's take that step now.

Step One

In a letter to the church in Rome, Paul made an amazing and rather gutsy confession.

> I do not understand my own actions. For I do not do what I want, but I do the very thing I hate. Now if I do what I do not want, I agree that the law is good. But in fact it is no longer I that do it, but sin that dwells within me. For I know that nothing good dwells within me, that is, in my flesh. I can will what is right, but I cannot do it. For I do not do the good I want, but the evil I do not want is what I do. Now if I do what I do not want, it is no longer I that do it, but sin that dwells within me.
>
> So I find it to be a law that when I want to do what is good, evil lies close at hand. For I delight in the law of God in my inmost self, but I see in my members another law at war with the law of my mind, making me captive to the law of sin that dwells in my members. Wretched man that I am! Who will rescue me from this body of death? (Romans 7:15-24)

I remember how these words leapt out at me the first time I read them. I felt as if I were looking into a giant mirror. Paul was not just describing himself, he was describing me.

In Robert Louis Stevenson's work *Jekyll and Hyde*, Dr. Jekyll was a good person, a respected physician, surrounded by friends who hated to leave his dinner parties because they enjoyed his company. So am I. I am a good person. My friends ask me to play golf. My adult children ask me for advice. My wife tells me she is blessed to have me not only as a husband, but also as her best friend. I am a good person. There is, however, another side of me, a Mr. Hyde. Another person lurks inside of me: a person I do not like, a person I try to hide. This person gets jealous of other's success. This person struggles with anger, an inner rage. This person silently cuts others down to feel better about himself. I do not like this person. This is not the person I want to be, and like the Apostle Paul, I sometimes feel like saying, "Wretched man that I am! Who will rescue me from this body of death?"

What Paul experienced, Bill W. described in the First Step: *We admitted we were powerless over [sin]—that our lives had become unmanageable.* Paul did what many hesitate to do. He took Step One. He admitted his powerlessness: "I can will what is right, but I cannot do it." Why did he take the First Step? Let me venture a couple of guesses.

The Myth of Control
First, Paul admitted he was powerless over sin because it was true.

We *are* powerless over sin, and left to our own resources, our lives *do* become unmanageable. We have grown up with a terrible myth: the myth of control. Our parents taught it to us, and we teach it to our children, and our children will teach it to their children. We all have heard the words: "Take charge. Be in control. Be strong. Be the master of your own destiny." Unfortunately, we have come to believe them. We believe that if we apply a little more willpower, if we just try a little harder, we can do it. We can change our troublesome behaviors. We can stop doing whatever we are doing.

Of course, not all control is bad. Self-control is certainly good. The Apostle Paul even lists it as a fruit of the Spirit: "love, joy, peace, patience, kindness, generosity, faithfulness, gentleness, and *self-control*" (Galatians 5:22-23). We like it when parents control their children in restaurants and dog owners control their dogs when walking through neighborhoods. We also like to know that at an altitude of thirty thousand feet, our pilot is in control of the plane. Not all control is bad. Some control is good. However, when we think we can gain control of everything, including our sin, we enter into the realm of delusional thinking.

I think of the fable about a big-headed lion who convinced himself he was the supreme ruler of all he surveyed. The lion strutted around the jungle asking, "Who is the king of the jungle?"

The little mouse answered, "You are, sir."

The rabbit answered, "You are, sir."

The monkey, the giraffe, the leopard, the ocelot, the wildebeest all answered the same. Then he approached the elephant. He roared his question, "Who is the king of the jungle?" and the elephant proceeded to wrap his trunk around him, twirl him over his head, and send him crashing to the ground. The lion got up, woozy and dazed, and wobbled back to the elephant. He looked the elephant in the eye and said, "You don't have to get sore because you do not know the right answer."

We are so much like that lion. We are so sure we are in control. We are certain we are the king or the queen of our jungle. If only we could diffuse that myth and face the truth. We *are* powerless over sin, and without supernatural intervention, our lives *do* become unmanageable.

Of course, when it comes to a problem behavior or practice, some say, "It is not all that bad. I can stop anytime I want." Sometimes we do. Sometimes we give up "sweets" for a period of time. Sometimes we start driving the speed limit after multiple speeding tickets. Sometimes we stop sleeping late by going to bed earlier. We think because our will is sufficient to change some things, we can change all things. Not true. Some things we cannot manage by ourselves.

If you think you can change and manage all things, try this little experiment. Think of some behavior you would like to stop. What would it be? Lying? Smoking? Drinking? Exaggerating? Sleeping around? People pleasing? Eating excessively? Spending impulsively? Working obsessively? Cleaning compulsively? Raging uncontrollably? Talking incessantly? Criticizing constantly? Whatever it is, do you have it in mind? Okay then, stop it! Stop lying. Stop smoking. Stop drinking. Stop exaggerating. Stop sleeping around. Stop tiptoeing around people. Stop eating more than your body needs. Stop buying things on credit. Stop working unreasonably long hours. Stop vacuuming. Stop flying off the handle. Stop always having to put in your two cents. Stop criticizing others. Stop! Just stop!

Do you see the problem? We cannot always *will* ourselves to change. Some behaviors we cannot stop, no matter how hard we try. They are unmanageable, and like the Apostle Paul, we want to do what is good, but we can't pull it off.

For as long as I can remember, I have been a people pleaser. I make every effort to keep everyone happy. The only trouble is, "You can't please everyone," and when I disappoint or hurt someone or when someone dislikes me, I go into an emotional tailspin. As a result, I have developed this habit of becoming what others want me to become, so much so that I lose myself along the way. I become like those ancient Greek actors in the theater. Because people in the back rows of massive Greek amphitheaters could not see the actors' faces, the performers took to wearing giant masks and thus never revealed their true faces. I act like one of those performers. I put on mask after mask, becoming the "character" others want me to be . . . and I hate it . . . and I cannot stop it.

Oh, I've tried. It goes something like this: Get frustrated with myself for being such a people pleaser. Vow to act differently tomorrow. Do better for a week, and then do it again. Become angry at myself. Get silently angry at others for expecting too much of me. Get more determined to fix the problem. Have lunch with someone the next day and put on another mask. Get even angrier with myself. Get embarrassed that I cannot fix this even though I have been working on it for years. Vow to form a "People Pleaser Anonymous Group." Never go.

The Power of Confession

Second, Paul came clean because he knew the power of confession.

One time-honored way of dealing with our Mr. or Ms. Hyde self is to deny it. Think of the Apostle Peter on the night of Jesus's arrest. On the Mount of Olives, Jesus told the disciples what was to come: that he would be handed over to his enemies, and his disciples would desert him. In other words, Jesus was telling the disciples, and especially Peter, something about themselves that they did not want to hear. The thought of deserting a best friend in his hour of need is not something they wanted to acknowledge about themselves. So Peter vehemently denied it: "Oh no, Jesus, not me. Others may desert you, but not me. I will stick with you to the very end." Jesus replied, "Peter, that's not true. Before the rooster crows three times in the morning, you will have denied me."

When Peter denied his capacity to betray a friend, he actually empowered that very part of himself. Denial did not diffuse his capacity for betrayal, it fueled it. When we deny those aspects of ourselves we find too distasteful to admit, instead of getting rid of the objectionable aspects of ourselves, we simply turn them loose to roam at will. Had Peter been willing to face his cowardly self, he might have been able to mobilize the Dr. Jekyll part of him that really wanted to be faithful. Denial is never a good thing. Denial gets us into trouble by refusing to acknowledge trouble! Denial keeps us from facing the truth about ourselves so that we can deal with that truth. Author Keith Miller calls it "a form of repression through which people blot out certain aspects of their own behavior from their own view."[4] Denial says everything is fine when it is not. Denial ignores the great divide between what we say and who we are.

On the other hand, confession—admitting who we are—empowers us to become the people God intends us to be. It helps to come clean. It helps to admit we have a problem. Confessing invites God into the healing process and is the first step toward becoming spiritually whole. Confession involves two actions on our part. The first act of confessing is naming the problem. When we name what is getting the best of us, we take a step toward taming it. If you cannot think of an area of your life that is unmanageable, just listen to the people around you. They have been naming it for years.

A mother told a friend, "I might have a problem with anger when it comes to my kids. I am not a screamer. I don't physically spank them, but I am short with them, and I don't like my tone of voice when I interact with them." The friend did not say, "Gosh, we all do that. Don't worry about it." Instead she replied, "I see that in you. In fact, I've been trying to tell you that for years." If we listen to what family members and friends have been trying to tell us, we can begin to name those parts of ourselves that need significant attention.

The second act of confessing is admitting we are powerless over the problem. Granted, we may have periods of control, but the problem always returns like weeds to a garden. If we will not admit our powerlessness, we cannot grow spiritually. Regrettably, some have to "hit bottom" before they admit to their powerlessness, whether it's a woman who gets ticketed for driving while intoxicated, or a man whose wife walks out on him, or a student who flunks out of college, or an executive who gets fired from a job. Often it takes a jolt to awaken us to the fact that our life has become unmanageable, and we need help putting things back together. It does not, however, need to be that way. We do not have to "hit bottom." We can take action before it gets that far. We can say, "Hold on. I need help here," to whatever plagues us, no matter how big or how small it may be.

In the Sermon on the Mount Jesus said, "Blessed are the poor in spirit, for theirs is the kingdom of heaven" (Matthew 5:3). One biblical scholar translates that as, "Blessed are the desperate." With nowhere else to turn, they just may turn to Jesus. In a counter-intuitive fashion, Jesus saw the powerless and the desperate, as having an advantage over the rest of us. They are blessed because they realize they are not self-sufficient. They are blessed because they may reach out to the one who can do something about the specific sin they battle. Also, note that Jesus did not say, "Blessed are those who were once spiritually poor and now have it all together." Rather he said, "Blessed are the poor in spirit," which suggests this inner poverty should remain constant. We do not grow out of this need for help. Whether we are the Pope or someone in a pew, we never stop saying to Christ, "I can't, but you can." To move beyond powerlessness is to move in the wrong direction.

Let us not forget the lesson of the little white mouse. A man purchased a white mouse to feed his pet snake. He dropped the unsuspecting mouse into the snake's cage, where the snake was sleeping in a bed of sawdust. The tiny mouse had a serious problem on his hands. At any moment he could be swallowed alive. Obviously, the mouse needed to come up with a brilliant plan. What did the terrified creature do? He quickly began covering the snake with sawdust chips until it was completely buried. With that, the mouse apparently thought he had solved his problem. The solution, however, came from outside. The man took pity on the silly little mouse and removed him from the cage.

No matter how hard we try to cover up or deny our battle with sin, it's fool's work. Sin will eventually awake from sleep and shake off its cover. Were it not for the saving grace of God's hand, sin would eat us alive.

We need to admit we are powerless over sin and that our lives have become unmanageable.

Summary Points to Ponder

- *The Twelve Steps have deep roots in the Christian faith.*

- *God uses the Twelve Steps to relieve suffering, fill emptiness, and foster emotional, relational, mental, and spiritual renewal.*

- *We never finish working the Twelve Steps.*

- *The Twelve Steps build upon one another.*

- *Step One describes the human condition: We are powerless over sin and our lives have become unmanageable.*

- *We have grown up with a terrible myth: the myth of control.*

- *Denial gets us into trouble by refusing to acknowledge trouble.*

- *If we will not admit our powerlessness, we cannot grow spiritually.*

- *Whether we are the Pope or someone in a pew, we never stop saying to Christ, "I can't, but you can." To move beyond powerlessness is to move in the wrong direction.*

Personal Exercise

1. List behaviors you would like to change. It may be your eating habits. It may be your spending habits. It may be your temper. It may be your negativity. It may be your fudging the truth to portray yourself in a better light. It may have to do with your sexuality. If you can't think of anything that needs changing, ask someone who knows you well what they would like to see you change.

2. List people over whom you feel powerless: people in your family, at work, at church, on the block. What behaviors in them irritate you? What is it they do that you can't get them to quit doing? What, if any, of those irritating behaviors may be in you?

Group Discussion and Sharing

1. What did you "cover up" from your parents when you were a child?

2. Share three significant steps—other than marriage and children—you have taken in your life.

3. Where do you feel you have things "in order" or seemingly "under control"?

4. What area(s) of your life appear(s) to be unmanageable?

5. What would you like to see happen as a result of this study?
    a. Get more honest with myself and others.
    b. Learn more about the Twelve Steps.
    c. Draw closer to others.
    d. Get a handle on the thorny places in my life.
    e. Experience God more fully.
    f. Take a step toward wholeness.
    g. Other.

Chapter 2

"Help, I Need Somebody"

Step Two: We came to believe that a Power greater than ourselves could restore us to sanity.

Ever go to camp as a child? My first camping experience was as an adult, at a YMCA camp on Catalina Island. During my freshman year at UCLA, I coached fourth-grade boys in a YMCA sports league, and the Y asked if I would consider counseling these boys at summer camp. I agreed, not knowing what I was getting myself into. It turned out to be one of the most exhausting weeks of my life. I counted the days until I could get back home.

I did, however, enjoy the evening campfire. Each night we performed skits, listened to talks, and sang songs: serious songs and silly songs . . . "Bill Grogan's Goat" . . . "Row, Row, Row, Your Boat" . . . "Little Bunny Foo Foo" . . . "Duke of York" . . . "John Jacob Jingleheimer

Schmidt" . . . "'Dem Bones" . . . "The Froggie Song" . . . "Do Your Ears Hang Low?" . . . "Wattleatcha" . . . and my theme song for my first week at camp, "Boom Boom, Ain't It Great to Be Crazy." The verses escape me, but the chorus has stayed with me for years:

> Boom, boom, ain't it great to be crazy?
> Boom, boom, ain't it great to be crazy?
> Giddy and foolish the whole day through
> Boom, boom, ain't it great to be crazy?

Contrary to the message of that little song, it's *not* "great to be crazy." Our images of craziness or "insanity" are, for the most part, very unpleasant. Our minds go to the movie *One Flew Over the Cuckoo's Nest*. We think of people locked away in institutions, behaving wildly and uncontrollably, drooling at the mouth, sleeping in padded rooms. Or we picture people with glazed, empty expressions, unable to converse, reason, function, or behave with any sense of normalcy.

Based on these images of insanity, we would be quite normal. Let us, however, see how the dictionary defines "insanity." One dictionary defines it as "Relatively permanent disorder of the mind; Very foolish." Another dictionary reads, "When something is not sensible and is likely to have extremely bad results." Still another describes insanity as a "Persistent mental disorder or derangement." Parts of those definitions *do* apply to us. At least they apply to me. I can think of numerous times when I have acted foolishly or done something that had an extremely bad result. I have certainly done some things that do not make a lot of sense.

When we do things like this, usually we learn from our mistakes, change our behavior, and do not repeat it. To be "insane," however, requires more. It requires us to do the same foolish behavior again and again. Imagine, for example, that you stop at the new Exxon/Mobil gas station on your way home. You press the "credit outside" pad and insert a Shell Oil card. The LCD monitor on the gas pump says, "Card Not Acceptable." You realize what you have done. You've mistakenly pulled out the wrong credit card and tried to pay for Exxon/Mobil gas with a Shell card. You retrieve your Exxon/Mobil card and finally get your gas.

A week later you pull into the same Exxon/Mobil gas station. Once again you press "credit outside" on the pump, and once again you pull out your Shell Oil card to pay for the gas. The LCD monitor reads, "Card Not Acceptable." So you reach into your wallet and pull out your Exxon/Mobil card and begin filling your tank.

Now imagine you keep doing this week after week. Every week you pull out the Shell Oil card instead of the Exxon/Mobil card. Every week the monitor reads "Card Not Acceptable." Every week you have to reach back into your wallet for the correct card. That would be "insane" behavior. Doing the same foolish thing again and again and expecting different results does not make any sense. That would constitute a "persistent mental disorder."

Step Two

Step Two reads: *We came to believe that a Power greater than ourselves could restore us to sanity.*

What does it mean to be "sane"? One dictionary defines "sanity" as "Soundness of reason or judgment." Another dictionary defines it as "Soundness of health of mind." Still another defines it as "The condition of being mentally healthy and able to make rational decisions."

So how are we doing in the sanity department? We are probably doing pretty well. We probably operate with a 95-5 sanity-insanity ratio, acting sanely 95 percent of the time and insanely only 5 percent of the time. Or maybe it's more like 90-10 or 80-20, but not enough to make us "certifiably insane." Somewhere in our lives, however, we do need to be restored to sanity. We do need to work on that 5, 10, or 20 percent of ourselves that is driving us and our friends and family crazy. In some areas we do suffer from an inability to reason soundly, logically, and to make consistently wise choices. In some areas of our lives, we keep doing the same thing, the same way, and expect different results.

Maybe it is the way we continue to use silence as a weapon to hurt others. Our relationships deteriorate when we do it, but we keep doing it. Maybe we eat sweets when trying to lose weight. We know that is not helping our diet, but we keep popping those chocolates and slices of Key Lime pie into our mouths. Maybe we are worry-aholics. We think that by worrying about events and people we might keep bad things from happening, but bad things still happen, and we are still miserable. Maybe we are compulsive talkers. We say to ourselves, "Next time I will ask questions and not give my opinion unless asked," but we keep blabbing away and wonder why people avoid us.

I am a constant cleaner. I do not tolerate clutter or messes. Our adult children kid me about it, especially when it comes to keeping the carpet clean. Something spills on the carpet and they say, "Dad, that looks like a one-treatment spill (or a two-treatment spill, or God forbid, a three-treatment spill)." I pull out the cleaner spray bottle like a gunslinger pulls out his pistol. I am lightning fast when it comes to cleaning up carpet spills. I once followed my son across the living room carpet when he had mud on his shoes. I said, "Josh, stop. Do not move." He stopped dead in his tracks. With spray bottle in hand, I told him, "Give me your shoes," just as an armed robber might say, "Give me your purse." I try to stop. I try to be less obsessive about clutter and messes, but I have not been able to do it. My children think I am "insane," "crazy," "mad" when it comes to cleaning.

Step One essentially focuses on the problem: We define our insanity; we identify recurring patterns of isolation or anger or procrastination or resentment; we acknowledge patterns of broken relationships; we recognize when we make rules we do not keep, or cut and run when things get tough, or have the desire to control situations and people. That leaves us with the question, "If we are powerless over sin, where can we find help?" The Second Step answers, "Your help comes from a Power greater than yourself. That Power can and will restore you to sanity."

The Big Book of AA reads:

> If a mere code of morals or a better philosophy of life were sufficient to overcome alcoholism, many of us would have recovered long ago. But we found that such codes and philosophies did not save us, no matter how much we tried. We could wish to be moral, we could wish to be philosophically comforted, in fact, we could will these things with all our might, but the needed power wasn't there. Our human resources, as marshaled by the will, were not sufficient; they failed utterly.

Lack of power, that was our dilemma. We had to find a power by which we could live, and it had to be a Power greater than ourselves.[5]

The Higher Power

At this point, some Christians raise objections. They do not like the "Higher Power" language used by some in AA. They say it compromises the gospel of Jesus Christ. I disagree. Think what would have happened if Step Two read, "We came to believe that Jesus Christ could restore us to sanity." While I may prefer that language, alcoholics who had trouble with the church certainly would not. They would immediately associate the name of Jesus with how the church had treated them and not consider Step Two. If the Steps included Christocentric language, the Steps would not have been so openly available to other faith traditions. Finally, atheists and agnostics certainly would have taken a pass. "Higher Power" language leaves the door open for all.

And Step Two is critical because without belief, healing does not happen. So the authors reasoned, "If we can just get people to believe in a Higher Power, without naming the Power, many will eventually get to Jesus Christ on their own." Even though one's "Higher Power" can be anything or anyone a person wishes, we must not forget that the word "God," with a capital "G," occurs 277 times in the third edition of AA's Big Book. (The Big Book written in 1939 stands today as the primary text for AA and is the foundation for most other Twelve Step programs.) Add to that the Big Book's use of biblical names for God such as "Creator," "Maker," "Heavenly Father," and the word "God" occurs over four hundred times.[6]

We must also keep in mind that AA did not invent the "Higher Power" language. In the New Testament there is a story about Bartimaeus that is helpful here. Jesus was on the last leg of his journey to Jerusalem, and he passed through Jericho some fifteen miles from the capital city. Passover was fast approaching, and the road was packed with pilgrims heading to the Holy City. Alongside the road was another crowd: parade watchers, curiosity seekers, and those too poor, too diseased, too physically challenged to make the journey to Jerusalem. Bartimaeus was a face in the crowd sitting along that roadside. He was not heading toward Jerusalem. He was blind and begging for money as people passed through town. When he heard that the miracle worker, Jesus, was passing by, Bartimaeus cried out, "Jesus, Son of David, have mercy on me." Immediately people around him tried to shut him up, but Bartimaeus would not be silenced. He knew his chance for healing was at hand, and he did not want to miss it. Jesus responded to this man's unsophisticated cry and gave him the gift of sight. Jesus healed him even though Bartimaeus had an underdeveloped picture of who Jesus was.

You see, Bartimaeus called Jesus "Son of David," not "Son of God" or "Son of Heaven." "Son of David" carried with it all the thought of a victorious Messiah, a king from David's line who would lead Israel to political and national prominence—but the Son of David was not divine. He was a man with greater power than Bartimaeus possessed, but the Son of David was still a man. That was a very inadequate picture of Jesus. Bartimaeus's concept of a "Higher Power" was not fully developed, but Jesus accepted Bartimaeus's picture of him. He knew Bartimaeus was a man in process, and most importantly Jesus reached out and healed him.

What made Bartimaeus well was trusting in a Power to heal him that was greater than his own power. That is the Second Step: coming to believe that a Power greater than ourselves can restore us to sanity.

Coming to Believe

"Coming to believe" means shifting our focus from a self-willed, "I'll decide what is right for me," and "I'll fix this myself," to the belief that Jesus Christ can give us perspective and strength to become more spiritually, relationally, mentally, physically, and emotionally whole. "Coming to believe" means reaching beyond ourselves and having faith that God can do for us what we cannot do for ourselves. "Coming to believe" also means wrestling with the part of ourselves that has trouble believing. Step Two requires a step of faith—not a big step, not a major step, but a step nonetheless.

A father brought his epileptic son to Jesus for healing (Mark 9:14-28). From the boy's birth his father had searched for a cure for his son's illness. He had done everything in his power to make his son well, but his power was not enough. He finally came to believe that a Power greater than himself would return his life and the life of his son to wholeness. When the man and his son arrived, Jesus was not present. He was on his way back from the Mount of Transfiguration. The disciples had tried to help. They had attempted to heal the boy, but had been unsuccessful. When Jesus arrived, the father pleaded with him, "If you are able do anything, have pity on us and help us." Jesus told the man, "If you are able! All things can be done for the one who believes."

The father replied, "I believe; help my unbelief!"

How much faith did the father possess? Not much. He had some, but not a lot. Paraphrasing what the father said might go something like this: "Jesus, I have this much faith. It's not much. If you are able—and I think you can, but I'm not sure—will you heal my boy? I wish I had more faith. Help me with my unbelief."

That's not a lot of faith, but Jesus does not require much faith. He said, "If you have faith the size of a mustard seed, you will say to this mountain, 'Move from here to there,' and it will move; and nothing will be impossible for you" (Matthew 17:20-21). The mustard seed was the smallest unit of measure in Jesus's time. Put in today's language it might read, "If you have the faith the size of a proton—or even a quark—you can move mountains." In other words, the *size* of our faith is not as important as the *object* of our faith. Where do we put our trust? In what do we believe? If the object of our faith is not worth a hill of beans, it does not matter how much faith we have. On the other hand, if the object of our faith can be trusted, if the object of our faith is reliable, a little dab of faith will suffice.

There was an American soldier held prisoner in North Vietnam who was led to believe that if he cooperated with his captors, he would be set free. He had all sorts of faith in his captors and did quite well, despite two years in captivity. With faith in his captors, he even became the leader of a prison thought-reform group. When he realized, however, that he was being deceived, he curled up on his bunk, refused nourishment, and died in a couple of weeks.

Faith is only as good as the object of our faith. If we believe that a certain chair will hold us when we sit on it, the primary issue is the construction and quality of the chair. Even if we believe very strongly that the chair will support us, if the chair is a rotten, broken-down piece of junk, it will still break if we try to sit on it. Our faith will not make the chair reliable. But if the chair is of quality construction, it takes very little faith to sit comfortably in it. It's the *quality* of the object, not the *quantity* of our faith, that is of primary importance.

I know some who read this may have difficulty trusting God, especially those who feel God has let them down in the past. They may have trusted, they may have put as little or as much faith as they had in God, and it seemed that God did not come through. Their spouse still walked out. The cancer did not go away. Their promotion did not come through. Mr. or Ms. Right never appeared. They asked, and they felt God turned a back to them. That happened to my wife, Trudy. A number of years ago, I had heart bypass surgery. It was one of those "if anything can go wrong, it will go wrong" type of surgeries. The surgery started with simple angioplasty, but a vein tore, and they rushed me upstairs for an emergency bypass procedure. Twelve hours later, they wheeled me back into the operating room to repair a leakage. Then a month after the surgery, doctors discovered some irregularities, and I had to go back to the hospital for additional measures. Over the course of that month, Trudy felt that with everything she prayed for, the opposite happened, so she stopped praying. She stopped praying for six months. It took awhile for her to trust God again.

For some it will take time to trust again. All they may be able to say at this point is, "I believe. Not much. Just a little. I'm afraid to get my hopes up. I do not want to be disappointed again, but I'll give it a try." But that's enough! Step Two requires a *step* of faith, not an entire marathon. For some of us, it will be a big step. For others, it will be a small step. But we do need to take that step and believe that a Power greater than ourselves can restore us to sanity.

Asking for Help

The evidence of our belief is in what we do next. We need to ask God for help. We need to ask God to restore us to sanity, and that might be another big step for some of us, especially if we are self-sufficient, autonomous, pull-ourselves-up-by-our-bootstraps people. Many of us do not like to ask for help, thinking it is a sign of weakness.

Remember Gordon Liddy, the Watergate conspirator? Today he hosts a nationally syndicated radio program, but at one time he played a key role in the Nixon White House. For his role in Watergate, and for refusing steadfastly to implicate others, Liddy was sentenced to over twenty years in prison. He served nearly five years, many in maximum security, including 106 days of solitary confinement, before his release by President Carter. When Liddy was released from prison he declared, "I have found within myself all that I need and all I shall ever need. I am a man of great faith, but my faith is in G. Gordon Liddy. I have never failed me." Talk about self-made. He even titled his autobiography *Will*. Some of us have similar tendencies, thinking that we can do it all ourselves, that we do not need help.

I love the story of the little girl who dressed up as Wonder Woman for her school's Halloween party. She was headed out the door to catch the school bus, and as she picked up her books and lunch box and moved toward the door, she exclaimed, "I'm Wonder Woman."

"Do you need any help carrying your things to the bus?" her mother asked.

"Oh, no," the little girl reiterated, "I'm Wonder Woman."

The mother waited for the sound of the front door closing behind her daughter, but instead she heard a tiny voice cry out, "Mommy, can you come here and tie my shoe?"

We may think we are Wonder Woman. We may think we are Superman. We think we can handle it on our own. We think we can do it ourselves. So we do not ask anyone for help; we tough it out. But to be delivered from our insane and broken behaviors, we need to ask for help. We need to ask someone bigger than ourselves to fix it. We need God.

Imagine if we attempted brain surgery on ourselves. It would be insane to try. We would kill ourselves trying to heal ourselves. When we need surgery, we must put ourselves in the hands of a skilled surgeon. Likewise, there are some things about ourselves we cannot fix. We need to ask God for help.

A Big Promise

"Ask, and it will be given you; search, and you will find; knock, and the door will be opened for you" (Matthew 7:7). This promise is as big as it gets! Can we trust this promise? Can we lean hard on it? Will it hold us up?

Theodore Parker Ferris, an Episcopal priest and author of eight books, preached a sermon titled "Revelation and Response" that began with these words:

> One time when I was speaking to people about God, I said that in the long run the real issue is between those who think that they are struggling against a universe that is meaningless at best, hostile at worst, and those who think that the universe makes sense, and that at heart it is friendly. That, to my way of thinking, is the real issue of the existence of God.[7]

Is the universe friendly? Is God friendly? Jesus answered, "Yes, I am. Yes, God is. Just ask, and it will be given to you." But we object. What about all the times we asked and nothing happened? How about all the times we asked and God was silent? What are we to do about that? Jesus answers, "Ask. Ask. Ask."

Ferris was not alone in thinking we live in a friendly universe. Richard Foster, a Quaker and founder of the church renewal organization Renovare, believes it as well:

> Do you know why the mighty God of the universe chooses to answer prayer? It is because his children ask. God delights in our asking. He is pleased at our asking. His heart is warmed by our asking.[8]

"Ask, and it shall be given to you." Ask what? Jesus does not say. He leaves the promise astonishingly open-ended. It is as if he were saying, "Take heart. You live in a friendly universe. God is on your side. The way to receive what you need from God is to ask. Just ask." The words of the old hymn come to mind: "Oh, what peace we often forfeit; Oh, what needless pain we bear—all because we do not carry everything to God in prayer." How many times have we talked only to ourselves about our problems? How many times have we tossed and turned at night because of worry? Jesus opens the door here and says, "You do not need to do this alone. You can ask for help with your problems and concerns. You will receive a warm audience." Could it be that Jesus is so dangerously absolute here about asking and receiving because of our proclivity of doing things on our own? He does not appear to be concerned about abuses and misunderstandings of prayer. He does not seem to be concerned with things like: What if God says "no"? What if God is silent? Jesus seems to be concerned only that we ask.

Some folks look down their noses at "asking" prayer. They contend that the real masters of the spiritual life go beyond asking to adoring God's nature, with no needs or requests whatsoever. They see asking prayer as a more crude form of prayer, whereas praise and adoration are more enlightened ways of communicating with God. This could not be further from the truth. We will never grow out of asking because we will always be dependent upon God. The Bible is full of asking prayer. The Lord's Prayer itself contains six petitions: Thy kingdom come; Thy will be done; give us our daily bread; forgive our sins/trespasses/debts; lead us not into temptation; and deliver us from evil. Jesus recommend this way of praying.

In 1998, forty-year-old Reynaldo Tovar-Valdivia was arrested for possessing methamphetamines with intent to distribute. Upon pleading guilty, he was sentenced to ten years in prison. In January 2000, his conviction was overturned when it was discovered that police had conducted an illegal search on the man's property. U.S. District Judge Howard Sachs signed an order releasing Tovar-Valdivia. But somehow the order was misplaced, so Tovar-Valdivia was incarcerated for two more years. In March 2002, Tovar-Valdivia wrote a letter to the judge calling attention to the oversight: "I would like to humbly request that this court make an order invalidating my conviction. Thanks for your time, and have a nice day." A few weeks later the judge, impressed by the polite letter, facilitated the prisoner's request.

If Tovar-Valdivia had not asked, he would still be in prison. We, too, need to ask. We need to believe that a Power greater than ourselves—a friendly Power—wants to and can restore us to sanity.

When the Apostle Paul wrote to the church in Corinth about what he called his "thorn in the flesh," Paul never named the thorn. Some think it was malaria, some epilepsy, some poor eyesight, some a constant critic, some a bad marriage, some think an addiction. Whatever it was, Paul asked God to help him with it. In response, God affirmed Paul with these words: "My grace is sufficient for you, for power is made perfect in weakness" (2 Corinthians 12:9). In other words, "Paul, you did the right thing. You admitted your weakness. You acknowledged your powerlessness. I do my best work with desperate, hurting people. Let's see what I can do about that thorny issue in your life." When Paul asked, he found God waiting for him.

Summary Points to Remember

⊘ *Insanity is doing the same thing over and over again and expecting different results.*

⊘ *Step One acknowledges that we are powerless over sin, but that leaves us with the question, "Where can we find help?" The Second Step answers, "Your help comes from a Power greater than yourself. That Power can and will restore you to sanity."*

⊘ *AA did not invent the "Higher Power" language. Jesus recognized and responded to the faith of people in process.*

⊘ *When we "come to believe," we shift our focus from a self-willed, "I'll decide what is right for me," and "I'll fix this myself," to the belief that Jesus Christ can give us perspective and strength to become more spiritually, relationally, and emotionally whole.*

⊘ *Step Two requires a step of faith—not a big step, not a major step, but a step nonetheless.*

⊘ *Faith is only as good as the object of our faith. It's the quality of the object, not the quantity of our faith, that is of primary importance.*

◉ We need to ask God to restore us to sanity, and that might be a big step for some of us, especially if we are self-sufficient, autonomous, pull-ourselves-up-by-our-bootstraps people.

◉ We will never grow out of asking because we will always be dependent upon God.

◉ God assures us that "My grace is sufficient for you, for power is made perfect in weakness."

Personal Exercise

1. Meditate on the following passages:
   a. Matthew 7:7-11
   b. Luke 11:1-13
   c. Philippians 4:6-7

2. What is your present picture of God? What words would you use to describe this God: loving, caring, empathetic, distant, aloof, forgiving, hostile? *Benevolent, Compassionate, Divine, all-Powerful*

3. What would you like to ask of God today?
   Help me to prioritize; bring more peace, less chaos

Group Discussion and Sharing

1. Share a couple of events, persons, messages, or readings that have impacted your present view of God.

2. Where would you put yourself in the "coming to believe" department?
   a. Not even close to believing.
   b. Been there, done that.
   c. I do not want to be disappointed again.
   d. I believe in the group more than I do in God.
   e. I am taking baby steps in the faith and trust department.

f. I believe, help my unbelief.
g. What a friend we have in Jesus.
h. Other.

3. When have you been accused of being a little "crazy"? What was the "crazy" behavior? When have you thought or felt a little "crazy"?

4. What jumped out at you from this chapter? Why do you suppose it grabbed you? *Non-addictive behavior can be crazy behavior - being overscheduled*

5. How can the group be praying for you this coming week? *Pray that I can focus & prioritize my energies*

Doing too much; like right now. Being overwhelmed, I feel like I can't breathe. I'm not finding time for myself

My struggle with my schedule

Chapter 3

The Big Decision

Step Three: We made a decision to turn our wills and our lives over to the care of God *as we understood [God].*

Set in the Great Barrier Reef, the animated feature film *Find-*

ing Nemo recounts the comedic and eventful journeys of two fish. The fretful clownfish Marlin and his young son, Nemo, became separated from each another when Nemo was unexpectedly trapped by a deep-sea diver and thrust into a fish tank in a dentist's office overlooking Sydney Harbor. Buoyed by the companionship of a friendly but forgetful regal blue tang named Dory, the overly cautious Marlin embarked on a dangerous trek and found himself the unlikely hero of an epic journey to rescue his son.

In the process, Marlin and Dory got trapped in the mouth of a great whale. Fearing they would be swallowed, they hung onto the whale's tongue for dear life. In frustrated fury Marlin pounded on the whale's tendril cheeks until he fell—limp, worn, and dejected.

Dory sized up the situation differently. She had been trying to communicate with the whale the whole time, believing the whale could be trusted. She loosened her grip and encouraged Marlin to do the same, telling to him let go, reassuring him that everything would be okay.

When Marlin questioned how she knew this, her reply was simple: "I don't."

After a moment's hesitation, Marlin let go. They slipped down the whale's tongue, and moments later the whale sprayed them out of his spout into Sydney Harbor. Shortly after, they reunited with Nemo.[9]

Step Three

The first two Steps are about awareness and recognition. In Step One we become aware that our lives are out of control. In Step Two we recognize that we need to rely on something bigger than ourselves to help us change. The Third Step, however, asks more of us. Step Three asks us to let go—to let go of our need to control; to let go of our fear; to let go of our need to have it all figured out; to let go, and let God.

Step Three reads: We *made a decision to turn our wills and our lives over to the care of God* as we understood [God].

Making a decision does not sound too tough. After all, we make decisions all the time. You have made a number of them already today. You decided to get out of bed, what to have for breakfast, what to wear . . . even to read this chapter. Making decisions is not that difficult. But wait a minute. Look closely at what the Third Step asks us to decide. It asks us to make a decision to turn our wills and our lives over to the care of God. This Step does not ask us to turn over a *part* of our lives, or a little bit of our lives, or a single dimension of our lives to the care of God. No, the Third Step requires *all* of us. That's asking for much more. That's not like asking someone, "What do you want for breakfast?" Making a decision about our wills and our lives has major consequences . . . and it's scary. We may feel like Marlin peering down the whale's throat, wondering if we'll be "okay" if we let go. Will we be swallowed up or will we come to a good end? If we turn our lives over to God, can this God be trusted? If we turn our will over to God "as we understand" God, will this God take care of us?

As We Understand God

Step Three originally read, "We made a decision to turn our wills and our lives over to the care of God." Period. End of Step Three. No qualifying phrase *"as we understood"* God. That phrase was a later addition and somewhat of a compromise on Bill W.'s part.[10] The qualifying phrase makes sense. We all relate to God "as we understand" God. Relating to God is always deeply personal and filtered through our life experience, and understanding of God will differ from person to person. We may turn to the Scriptures for that understanding. We may turn to the person of Jesus Christ for that understanding. We may turn to the church for that understanding. But then we take that information, sift it through our brain cells, and come out with our understanding of God. Our understanding of God is never totally an objective comprehension; it is always somewhat subjective.

The qualifying phrase also gives us insight into why some have difficulty taking this Third Step. They easily climb Steps One and Two, but trip on Step Three. What trips them up? The problem is a distorted image of God. Sometimes we take our personal history and impose it on God. Some of us have replaced the face of God with the face of a father, or mother, or coach, or pastor, or teacher, or some other authority figure. Unfortunately, some of those people disappointed us. Some of those people hurt us. Some of those people did not keep promises. Some of those people let us down. So, we say, "I can't turn my will and my life over to God. God will let me down, just as my father (or mother, coach, pastor, teacher) did."

God's Care

While it may or may not alter our picture of God, let us go back in time to Jesus's feeding the five thousand. Hurt by the news of the death of his cousin John the Baptist, Jesus decided to get away by himself. The people, however, would not leave him alone. They followed him to the other side of the lake. Matthew tells us,

Now when Jesus heard this, he withdrew from there in a boat to a deserted place by himself. But when the crowds heard it, they followed him on foot from the towns. When he went ashore, he saw a great crowd; and he had compassion for them and cured their sick. (Matthew 14:13-14)

Good thing the crowd came to Jesus and not to me! If it had been me, that last sentence would have read, "When Richard went ashore, he saw a great crowd; and he cussed under his breath and curtly told them to 'go home. I need some time alone.'"

After hearing about the death of a family member, I would have been in no mood to preach, or teach, or care for the sick. Jesus probably wasn't either. After all, he *had* tried to get away from the crowds. He seemed to prefer being alone than dealing with the crowds. So why did he take time for them? Matthew tells us because "he had compassion for them."

Compassion is an important New Testament word. The Gospels often speak of Jesus as having it and being moved to it:

When he saw the crowds, he had *compassion* for them, because they were harassed and helpless, like sheep without a shepherd (Matthew 9:36).

When the Lord saw her, he had *compassion* for her and said to her, "Do not weep" (Luke 7:13).

So he set off and went to his father. But while he was still far off, his father saw him and was filled with *compassion*; he ran and put his arms around him and kissed him (Luke 15:20).

In the Old Testament the word usually translated as "compassion" is the plural of a noun that, in its singular form, means "womb." It connotes not only the origin of life, but also the origin of strong feelings. As a mother loves the children of her womb, so God loves us. The Greek word for compassion used in the story of the feeding of the five thousand is *splanchnizomai*, which literally means the "inward parts" of a human body. In today's vernacular we would translate it as "guts." Etymologically speaking, the English word "compassion" comes from two Latin words: *passion,* which means "to feel," and *com,* which means "with." Putting both words together, compassion literally means "to feel with passion." Compassion involves feeling the feelings of somebody else in a visceral way, not just in our head, but in our gut. Therefore, in writing that Jesus had compassion, Matthew was not saying that Jesus felt casual pity, but that Jesus strongly and intensely felt their pain. Above all else, this passage reminds us that Jesus/God cares.

When Dory told Marlin everything would be okay, Marlin wondered if the whale really did have his best interests in mind. When Dory encouraged Marlin to let go, Marlin wondered if the whale could be trusted. The big, powerful whale could have just as well consumed them as rescued them. Marlin knew the power of the whale. He knew the whale could help, but would it? The issue for Marlin was, "Does the whale care?"

We wonder the same about God. Does God care? If we are going to let go, we better be sure there is someone there who will catch us and not disappoint us. We better be sure this God feels our pain, understands our predicament, and has compassion for us. If this God does, then we can seriously consider turning our wills and our lives over to God's compassionate care.

Turning Over Our Wills and Lives

A wise man remarked, "There is a world of difference between existing and living." To exist simply means to have a beating heart and breathing lungs. To live, on the other hand, means to experience joy, wholeness, excitement, fulfillment, and peace. Jesus tells us how to *live,* not just exist.

> Then Jesus told his disciples, "If any want to become my followers, let them deny themselves and take up their cross and follow me. For those who want to save their life will lose it, and those who lose their life for my sake will find it. For what will it profit them if they gain the whole world but forfeit their life? Or what will they give in return for their life?" (Matthew 16:24-26)

The word Jesus used here for life was *psyche*, not *bios*. He was speaking not about our physical life but about our soul or inner life. He was essentially saying, "Disown the lordship of your own thinking and go under new management." He was telling us that the things we usually do to protect our inner self—manipulation, control, managing others, playing it safe—will actually destroy us. It's like the author of Proverbs said: "Sometimes there is a way that seems to be right, but in the end it is the way to death" (16:25).

The key to living and not just existing lies in the Third Step: By giving up our life, we get our life back. This involves three major actions on our part: surrender, patience, and perseverance.

Surrender

Most of us can identify with the person described in AA's Big Book:

> Each person is like an actor who wants to run the whole show; is forever trying to manage the lights, the ballet, the scenery, and the rest of the players in his own way. If his arrangements would only stay put, if only people would do as he wishes, the show would be great. Everybody, including himself, would be pleased. Life would be wonderful. In trying to make arrangements our actor may sometimes be quite virtuous. He [or she] may be kind, considerate, patient, generous; even modest and self-sacrificing. On the other hand, he may be mean, egotistical, selfish, and dishonest. But as with most humans, he is likely to have varied traits.
>
> What usually happens? The show doesn't come off very well. He begins to think life doesn't treat him right. He decides to exert himself more. He becomes, on the next occasion, still more demanding or gracious, as the case may be. Still the play does not suit him. Admitting he may be somewhat at fault, he is sure that other people are more to blame. He becomes angry, indignant, self-pitying. Is he not a victim of the delusion that he can wrest satisfaction and happiness out of this world if he only manages well? Is it not evident to all the rest of the players that these are the things he wants? And do not his actions make each of them wish to retaliate, snatching all they can get out of the show? Is he not, even in his best moments, a producer of confusion rather than harmony?[11]

Surrender releases us from the temptation of putting ourselves and our needs at the center of the universe and from the belief that everyone and everything revolves around us . . . even God! Many of us live our lives as if God were our servant and will help us attain our goals. When we pray, "Lord, help me with this or that," we sometimes fall into the trap of asking God to bless what we want without considering that this request may or may not be God's desire. In our denial we have the delusion that we are praying for God's will.

I can recall praying, "God, Trudy and I would really like to buy this house. Please keep it on the market until our current house sells. If someone else buys it, we know it was your will." Well, someone else bought the house and I was ticked . . . and exposed! If I had really been seeking God's will, if I had actually surrendered to God, I would not have been upset with God when we did not get the house. When someone else bought it, I would have said, "Well, God, you know what's best. May your will be done." Instead, I felt as if God had let us down. Unconsciously, I had fully expected God to do my bidding and get us that house! I had made a "conditional" surrender. But surrendering means handing the steering wheel over to someone else. As long as God did my bidding, I allowed God to take the wheel, but one wrong turn, and I wanted the steering wheel back.

Patience
Sometimes we have the mistaken idea that once we surrender to God, all our lifestyle issues will be magically solved. But surrender is not enough. We also need to be patient . . . with God and ourselves.

Tom Smith, trainer of the legendary horse Seabiscuit, knew horses. Based on his "almost mythical communion with them,"[12] millionaire Charles Howard was persuaded to purchase Seabiscuit. Seabiscuit was a horse whose physical shortcomings and temperament made him an unlikely prospect for racing success. Seabiscuit was not tall, sleek, and tapered, but rather short, rectangular, and rude. His gait was so out of whack that one observer said he waddled like a duck. At the age of three, Seabiscuit had run forty-three races, far more than most horses run in their entire careers, but he had not won any of them.

Then Smith hired a down-on-his-luck jockey named John "Red" Pollard to ride him. Red was considered too tall to be anything but a bush-league jockey and seemed a bad match for this undersized horse, but Smith noticed a numinous connection between Red and Seabiscuit. Red had another handicap: He was blind in one eye, a fact he had concealed, knowing that his riding career would be over if it were discovered.

During a crucial race at Santa Anita, however, Red's limited vision allowed a competing horse to overtake Seabiscuit on Red's blind side, costing them the victory. Smith was outraged and pressed the jockey to explain how he could have let this happen. It was then that Red revealed, "Because I'm blind!" Stung by the loss and betrayal, Smith urged Howard to fire Red. To Smith's surprise, Howard requested that Red remain as his jockey. When Smith demanded a reason, Howard said, "You don't throw away a whole life just because it's banged up a bit."

All of us are banged up a bit, but we are not permanently ruined. All of us can be improved, but it will take time. Surrendering to God will not bring an immediate cure. Over the years we will discover blind spots that we did not know we had, but God will not throw us away. God will be patient with us, and hopefully we will be patient with ourselves.

A man was visiting his daughter's home when his grandson grabbed his hand to take him to see something. The grandson had found a robin's egg in the backyard. With the help of his mother, the little boy had made a cotton nest under a lamp and placed the egg in it. They had researched what the temperature should be and had placed a thermometer to check it. They intended to watch the egg hatch.

His daughter had placed a card in front of this little experiment that read, "Shh, I'm happening!"

We need a sign like that. Every time we looked at it, we would be reminded to say to ourselves, "I am still happening. I'm not there yet, and I'm going to have some slipups in the process, but God will never give up on me—and I will never give up on myself. Yes, I'm banged up, but God sees more in me than I see in myself."

Perseverance

Our "happening" will take time. There will be no quick fix, no instant transformation. It will take the rest of our lives. Turning our lives over to God is not something we do once and for all. Rather, we do it repeatedly as we encounter new blind spots and repeat old behaviors. So we need to persevere.

An old evangelist had the right idea. He said, "Listen, I'm against sin. I'll kick it as long as I've got a foot. I'll fight it as long as I've got a fist. I'll butt it as long as I've got a head. And I'll bite it as long as I've got a tooth, and when I'm old, fistless, footless, and toothless, I'll gum it till I go home to glory and it goes home to perdition." The old evangelist did not expect a quick fix. He knew battling his inner demons would take a lifetime, but he was determined to win that battle.

Sir Edmund Hillary made several unsuccessful attempts at climbing Mount Everest before he finally succeeded. At one point he shook his fist at the mountain and said, "I'll defeat you yet, because you are as big as you're going to get, but I'm still growing."[13] His threat was prophetic. After repeated setbacks, he eventually climbed that mountain.

We will as well. As we work the Steps, we will make progress. We may not progress as quickly as we would like, but molecule by molecule, cell by cell, God will keep transforming us.

The House

At this point you might wonder, "Aren't these three Steps enough? Why do I need nine more Steps? If I turn my life over to God's care and commit myself to this process of repeatedly surrendering to God, why do I need to do anything more?"

Think of it this way. Suppose I meet my wife, Trudy, for lunch. Trudy is a real estate broker. She has sold houses for fifteen years and now manages a large residential sales office with over ninety agents. Over lunch I say, "Trudy, let's sell our house and buy a house on a golf course (I did suggest that at one time!). That way I can roll out of bed, get in a golf cart, and play golf as much as I want. Wouldn't that be heaven?"

Even if she agreed to something as crazy as that, we certainly could not move that afternoon. We would have to do a number of things between making the decision and actually moving into the house on the golf course.

First, we would get a market analysis of our home so we would know what it was worth. Second, we would list the house. (We would never go the "For Sale By Owner" route. If I even suggested selling our home without a realtor, I would be sleeping on the couch for a month!) Then we would begin our search for a house on a golf course. After finding the house, we would secure a bank loan. We'd do a title search of the new home and get the home inspections and appraisals. Then, finally, we would close on both houses.

We go through a similar process in the Third Step. We make a decision to "buy the house" by choosing to turn our wills and lives over to God, but we have not completed the transaction when we say those words. There is a lot to do before we move into the new house God has in mind for us.

What, then, gets us "into the house"? If surrendering our lives to God does not make us the people we want to be, then how do we do it? We do it by working all Twelve Steps. The rest of the Steps get us into the house. The remaining Steps make us, with God's help, into the persons we want to be. Spiritual renewal is a process. There are Twelve Steps to wholeness, not just three. Once we have decided to give our lives and wills over to God, the remaining Steps—Four through Twelve—help us to grow spiritually.

If we stop with Step Three, it's like deciding to buy a house, getting a realtor, applying for a loan, doing a "walk through," and stopping there. We do not close the deal. We do not move into the house. Likewise, we never move into being the new creation Christ intended us to be if we stop with the Third Step.

But, we are getting ahead of ourselves. Step Three is a crucial Step. We cannot get to the other Steps without taking this one.

Summary Points to Ponder

◈   *Step Three asks us to let go: to let go of our need to control; to let go of our fear; to let go of our need to have it all figured out; to let go, and let God.*

◈   *Relating to God is always deeply personal and filtered through our life experience.*

◉ *As a mother loves the children of her womb, so God loves us.*

◉ *By giving up our life, we get our life back.*

◉ *Surrender releases us from the temptation of putting ourselves and our needs at the center of the universe.*

◉ *We need a sign that reminds us to say to ourselves, "I am still happening. I'm not there yet, and I'm going to have some slipups in the process, but God will never give up on me—and I will never give up on myself."*

◉ *Turning our lives over to God is not something we do once and for all. Rather we do it repeatedly as we encounter new blind spots and repeat old behaviors.*

Personal Exercises

1. Make a list of all the decisions you made yesterday or today. Divide them into three columns: easy, moderate, and difficult.

2. Meditate on the following passages:
   a. John 3:1-21
   b. Romans 12:1-3
   c. Mark 12:28-30
   d. Galatians 2:20
   e. John 10:11-18

3. If you think you are ready to make the decision to turn your life and will over to God's care, recite this prayer of surrender:

   Dear God,
   I'm sorry about the mess I've made of my life. I want to turn away from all the wrongs I've ever done and all the wrongs I've ever been. Please forgive me for it all.

I know you have the power to change my life and can turn me into something new and beautiful. Thank you, God, for getting my attention long enough to interest me in trying it your way.

God, please take over the management of my life and everything about me. I am making this conscious decision to turn my will and life over to your care and am asking you to please take over all parts of my life.

Please, God, move into my heart. However you do it is your business, but make yourself real inside me and fill my emptiness. Fill me with your love and Holy Spirit and make me know your will for my life.

I rejoice that I am part of your people, and that you have control of my will and my life. I thank you and praise your name. Amen.

Group Sharing and Discussion

1. Share a relatively easy decision you made today.

2. As you reflect back on your life, what have been a couple of "agonizing" decisions you had to make?

3. What grabbed your attention from this chapter?

4. Step Three states: "We made a decision to turn our wills and our lives over to God *as we understood [God]*." Where are you with this decision?
   a. I'm still considering it.
   b. I'm a long way from it.
   c. I'm almost there.
   d. I made that decision awhile ago.
   e. I'm not sure if I really believe in a caring God.
   f. I need more information.
   g. Other.

5. Where do you particularly need to "let go and let God" this coming week?

Section Two

The Clean Up Steps

Though attributed to Benjamin Franklin, it was John Wesley who actually proclaimed, "Cleanliness is, indeed, next to godliness." This linking of cleanliness and godliness can be found earlier in the writings of Phinehas Ben Yair, one of the Hebrew fathers, who wrote, "The doctrines of religion are resolved into carefulness; carefulness into vigorousness; vigorousness into guiltlessness; guiltlessness into abstemiousness; abstemiousness into cleanliness; cleanliness into godliness."

Whether the quote originated with Franklin, Wesley, or Phinehas Ben Yair, I agree. I love cleanliness. I love cleaning. I enjoy washing clothes. I do not mind doing the dishes . . . and vacuuming is a little slice of heaven.

I know . . . not everyone feels the same. Some like getting dirt under their fingernails. Some like roughing it in the woods. Not me. I want to be within reach of a hot shower at all times.

Your feelings about cleanliness will no doubt affect your excitement about this next group of Steps. Steps Four through Seven ask us to clean up our insides—our attitudes and thoughts—and our outsides—our actions and behaviors. We begin in Step Four by taking a good, hard look at ourselves. We then move to Step Five and share what we have discovered about ourselves, both good and bad, with another person. In Step Six we prepare to ask God to remove our shortcomings, and then finally in Step Seven, we ask God to clean us up.

Step Four: We made a searching and fearless moral inventory of ourselves.

Step Five: We admitted to God, to ourselves, and to another human being the exact nature of our wrongs.

Step Six: We were entirely ready to have God remove all these defects of character.

Step Seven: We humbly asked [God] to remove our shortcomings.

Chapter 4

Making a List and Checking It Twice

Step Four: We made a searching and fearless moral inventory of ourselves.

A number of years ago Dorothy Alford, the owner of a local bookstore, gave me a wonderful book by Bonnie Sose titled *Talk to Me: 1777 Intimate Questions, Share Your Heart with a Loved One*. I have used the book in small groups, with friends, and especially with my wife. Even though Trudy and I have been married over thirty years, I learn new things about her every time we use this book. We take turns choosing a question to ask, and we share our answers during our morning walk. The book provides us with new opportunities to know, understand, and appreciate one another. I have heard her respond to questions such as:

"What qualities made you fall in love with your mate? What made you
   choose your mate over someone else? Give specific examples."
"How do you like to spend Sundays?"
"Name something you do strictly because it is important to your
   mate."
"How would you like to be cared for by your mate?"

I have chosen questions 739 and 1260 for upcoming walks: "What
do you really hate to be nagged about?" and "Can you recall the very
lowest point in your life?" The most recent edition of the book contains
2507 intimate sharing questions. We will be buying that one soon.

After asking Trudy over a thousand questions from the book, I have
come to know her quite well. She also knows a lot about me. In fact,
I know Trudy better than I know any other human being, and Trudy
knows me better than anyone else as well. But as much as we know
about each other, our knowledge pales in comparison to how well God
knows us.

Listen to the words of the psalmist:

O LORD, you have searched me and known me.
You know when I sit down and when I rise up;
You discern my thoughts from far away.
You search out my path and my lying down,
and are acquainted with all my ways.
Even before a word is on my tongue,
O LORD, you know it completely. (Psalm 139:1-4)

The Ultimate Know It All

God is the ultimate "know it all." There is nothing that God does not know
about us. This knowledge often leads to two opposite feelings. On the one
hand, knowing how well God knows us might make us afraid, especially if
we have something to hide. We may feel like the pastor who attended the
theater. His church deemed theater going sinful, but he wanted to see the
play, so he wrote the lead actor asking him if there was a back or side door
in the theater where he could slip in and out unnoticed. The actor wrote

back to the pastor, "My dear man, there is no door in my theater through which God cannot see."

That's what the psalmist was saying. There is no door in our theater, no door in our homes, no door in our office, no door in our leisure, through which God cannot see. Realizing God's omniscience and omnipresence can have an unsettling affect, so unsettling that we might be tempted to run away from such an all-knowing God. The psalmist, however, says it won't work. We cannot get away.

> Where can I go from your spirit?
> Or where can I flee from your presence?
> If I ascend to heaven, you are there;
> if I make my bed in Sheol, you are there. (Psalm 139:7-8)

When I was a child, I received an Ant Farm. It had a couple of pieces of clear plastic about a half an inch apart, and you filled the space between the sheets of plastic with dirt. Then you sent away for ants, and when they arrived, you put them in the farm and watched them dig elaborate tunnels under the surface of the dirt. I loved watching the ants do their ants' thing. Though perhaps a crude analogy, I think this is a little like it is with God. When we think we have gone underground and no one can see us, God can. Such scrutiny may be unsettling, but it wasn't for the psalmist. Instead, the psalmist found God's knowledge of our comings and goings, our thoughts and feelings, comforting.

> You hem me in, behind and before,
> and lay your hand upon me.
> Such knowledge is too wonderful for me;
> it is so high that I cannot attain it. (Psalm 139:5-6)

How can that knowledge be wonderful? How can we be comforted by the fact that God knows everything about us?

Have you had a child make you something in school? You might proudly display your child's handmade trivet, but in fact, it might be pretty ugly. It doesn't match the décor of the house. It's not a great work of art, but you use it. It sits on the stove, and you love it. Why?

Because you know your child wanted to make the best trivet he or she could make to please you.

Think of it this way: If we have taken the Third Step and turned our wills and our lives over to the care of God, God knows we want to change. God knows our desire to live differently. When our outward behavior is not in sync with our desire, when we "blow it" and fall short, *then* it is comforting that God knows everything about us. God knows our real desire is to put a smile on God's face. God knows we want to please our Creator.

Step Four

The psalmist found God's knowledge of him so comforting that he asked God's help in taking his Fourth Step. Note the psalmist's startling and courageous request:

> Search me, O God, and know my heart;
> test me and know my thoughts.
> See if there is any wicked way in me,
> and lead me in the way everlasting. (Psalm 139:23-24)

The Fourth Step reads: *We made a searching and fearless moral inventory of ourselves.* That's exactly what the psalmist wanted God's help in doing. The psalmist wanted to be God's person at any cost, so he invited God to make a thorough examination of him. He asked God to search him. The Hebrew word literally means "explore, dig, probe." The psalmist wanted God to penetrate his being, dig down within him, and reveal anything that needed fixing.

A number of years ago my sister and brother-in-law (Deb and Dick) took on a project for a little extra spending money. Once a month they went to an Arby's restaurant, ordered a meal, ate, and critiqued the restaurant. The Arby's fast-food chain had hired them to search out, probe, and explore the restaurants in order to find out anything that was keeping Arby's from becoming the best fast-food restaurant chain in the business. To test Arby's, Deb and Dick did different things. Sometimes they would act spacey. They would order something and then change their minds.

Sometimes they would act demanding. Sometimes they would be gruff and surly. They did different things to see how the Arby's staff treated them. They also checked to see if the restaurant was clean and attractive, and that the food was prepared and served in a timely fashion. Every time they did this, they received a free meal and $25. Their job was to search Arby's and to point out where Arby's could do better.

The psalmist asked God to do something similar: "Examine me. I can take it. Be honest. I want to know what I need to eliminate from my life. I do not want to miss anything. Look under the hood. Reveal to me what brings you pain." Such honesty puts us in touch with the truth about ourselves, and as Jesus promised, "The truth will make you free" (John 8:32).

Seek God's Protection and Assurance

Because of the deeply personal and radical honesty of the Fourth Step, however, we need to keep certain guidelines in mind as we embark upon it. First, before taking this Step, we need to ask God to protect us and assure us. The order of the Twelve Steps is not haphazard. A belief in a caring God to whom we have surrendered our wills and our lives is essential. An honest look at ourselves can be traumatic. We will see things we do not like. Some of those things may shock us. Some may hurt us. We may be in danger of sinking into despair. As a result, we need God's protection.

The psalmist wrote, "He will cover you with his pinions, and under his wings you will find refuge" (Psalm 91:4). That image reminds me of the forest ranger who, after a forest fire in Yellowstone National Park, found a bird petrified in ashes, perched statuesquely on the ground at the base of a tree. Somewhat sickened by the eerie sight, he knocked over the bird with a stick, and three tiny chicks scurried from under the dead mother's wings. The loving mother, keenly aware of impending disaster, had carried her offspring to the base of the tree and had gathered them under her wings, instinctively knowing that the toxic smoke would rise. She could have flown to safety but had refused to abandon her babies. When the blaze had arrived and the heat had singed her small body, the mother remained steadfast.

As the flames of radical self-examination engulf us, we need similar protection. We need God's assurance. I know when I "blow it" with Trudy, I need reassurance. I find myself asking her, "Do you still love me? Will you ever forgive me? You won't leave me, will you?" I abhor the way I acted and cannot imagine anyone could still love me, flaws and all. When we are working on Step Four, we need to remember that nothing can separate us from the love of God in Christ Jesus. If "neither death, nor life, nor angels, nor rulers, nor things present, nor things to come, nor powers, nor height, nor depth, nor anything else in creation will be able to separate us from the love of God" (Romans 8:38-39), then certainly our sins will not either.

Write It Down

In AA's Big Book we read, "In dealing with resentments, we set them on paper. . . . We reviewed our fears thoroughly. We put them on paper. . . . We reviewed our own conduct over the years past. . . . We got this all down on paper and looked at it."[14] What's the thinking behind this? Can't we just make a mental note of our shortcomings? Isn't that enough?

The reason for writing down our moral inventory becomes clear in the next Step. Step Five asks us to share our list with another human being! If we just run through an inventory in our minds, we may forget some things when we share it with a trusted friend or confidante. Putting our inventory on paper also makes it concrete and real in a way mere reflection does not.

Record the Good and the Bad

Making a moral inventory is not an exercise in character assassination. This is an *inventory* we are taking, and most every business person understands the need for an inventory from time to time. As the Big Book states, "A business which takes no regular inventory goes broke. Taking a commercial inventory is a fact-finding and fact-facing process."[15] During an inventory, the owner and the employees go into a store, factory, or warehouse and identify the good merchandise in stock as well as the out-of-date or damaged merchandise that needs to be taken off the shelves.

In Step Four we do the same thing with our lives. We take stock. We take an inventory of hurts we've inflicted, as well as people we have helped. We take stock of our self-defeating behaviors and our self-actualizing behaviors. We search for good moral behavior as well as inappropriate behavior. We record those aspects of our thoughts, feelings, attitudes, and behaviors we want to keep, as well as those we need to discard. We make sure we name qualities that others appreciate and for which they have affirmed us. Maybe we have a great laugh and bring joy to those around us. Maybe we listen well, and because of that, people feel valued when they are in our presence. Maybe we are dependable, trustworthy, patient, kind, gentle, or merciful. We need to include the good with the not-so-good.

Be Specific

When explaining something to others, we occasionally hear, "Could you be more specific?" The request for specificity is a request for better understanding. The same applies to taking our inventory. The more specific we can be during our inventory, the better. Generalities such as, "Sometimes I have trouble holding onto money" are not enough. Specifics such as "Six months ago I bounced two checks," or "I went on a buying spree last month at Nordstrom's" are more like it. If we list ten particular instances under the category of "lying," four under the category of "stealing," seven under the category of "greed," and five under the category of "generosity," we will have a sharper understanding of who we are.

Make It Personal

When we are taking our moral inventory, we need to make sure we are taking our own inventory and not someone else's. Jesus made this clear in the Sermon on the Mount.

> Do not judge, so that you may not be judged. For with the judgment you make you will be judged, and the measure you give will be the measure

you get. Why do you see the speck in your neighbor's eye, but do not notice the log in your own eye? Or how can you say to your neighbor, 'Let me take the speck out of your eye', while the log is in your own eye? You hypocrite, first take the log out of your own eye, and then you well see clearly to take the speck out of your neighbor's eye. (Matthew 7:1-5)

According to Jesus, our relation to others definitely conditions our relationship to God. Jesus linked our criticism of others to the criticism we will receive from God. Unfortunately, it's so much easier to focus on what someone else has done to us than focus on what we have done to others. It's so much easier to say, "Well, I did do this, but at least I'm not as bad as he or she is"; "I may have taken a couple of pens from the office, but at least I didn't embezzle money like she did"; or "I may have called in sick one day when I really wasn't, but he does it all the time"; or "I only lusted and fantasized over a person while he actually had an affair." When we undervalue the size of our own faults and overvalue the size of others', we do so at our own peril. In order to be healthy spiritually and emotionally, we need to shift the focus from "them" to us.

Distinguish False Guilt from Real Guilt

A sign in the window of a travel agency reads, "Ask us about our special Guilt Trip." We often take that trip needlessly. We feel guilty about things for which we should not feel guilty. For example, a friend asks if we can baby-sit tonight. We would rather not, and tell her so. We say, "We planned on a quiet night at home. We need the down time. We just do not have the energy to baby-sit tonight. Sorry. Ask us another time." Should we feel guilty? Absolutely not! We told the truth. We did not make up an excuse for not wanting to baby-sit. But *do* we feel guilty? Probably. That, however, is false guilt. False guilt is undeserved blame we take upon ourselves.

Real guilt, however, is another matter. Real guilt springs from being untrue to God, ourselves, and others. Real guilt pricks our conscience. Real guilt rightfully grabs our attention. It informs us that we have missed the mark and we need to apologize to someone, be it God, a friend, a spouse, a child, a neighbor, or a co-worker.

Take Your Time

The Fourth Step is not a Step to hurry through. Begin by writing down thoughts, feelings, attitudes, and behaviors—both good and bad—as they come to mind. Some memories will come quickly. Other memories will reveal themselves in time. As the author of Lamentations said, "Let us test and examine our ways, and return to the LORD" (3:40). The initial testing and examination may take days, weeks, even months.

Of course, asking God to shine the light of truth upon us is something we need to do throughout our lives. God, however, will reveal things to us only when we are ready to see them. Some things we will be ready to see and acknowledge today. Other matters God will leave for another season. Begin with what is clear. The important issue is not when you finish the inventory but that you start it.

Getting Started

There are several ways to get started with a moral inventory: the "Four Absolutes" approach, the "Sermon on the Mount" approach, or the "Seven Deadly Sins" approach. Consider each option and choose the one that seems most do-able for you.

The "Four Absolutes" Approach

Initially, Twelve Steppers measured themselves against the Oxford Group's "Four Absolutes": absolute honesty, absolute purity, absolute unselfishness, and absolute love. The Oxford Group borrowed the absolutes from Dr. Robert E. Speer's interpretation of Jesus's words, "Be perfect, therefore, as your heavenly Father is perfect" (Matthew 5:48). Speer drew "absolute honesty" from Jesus's words in John 8:44: "You are from your father the devil . . . [he] does not stand in the truth, because there is no truth in him. When he lies, he speaks according to his own nature, for he is a liar and the father of lies." Speer gleaned "absolute purity" from Jesus's words in Mark 7:15: "There is nothing outside a person that by going in can defile, but the things that come out are what defile." He patterned "absolute unselfishness" after the model of Jesus: "For the Son of Man came not to be served but to serve, and to give his life a ransom for many" (Mark 10:45). Finally, he took absolute love from Jesus's commandment: "I give you a new commandment, that you love one another. Just as I have loved you, you also should love one another" (John 13:34).[16]

If you choose to begin your moral inventory using these absolutes, here are some considerations that might help:

How are you doing when it comes to telling the truth?
Can you identify times you have lied to someone?
Have you ever exaggerated the facts or embellished a story?
What examples can you list of truth-telling and telling lies?

What about your commitment to purity?
Does your "thought life" ever get you into trouble?
Are there things about yourself you would be embarrassed if others knew?
Have you ever taken advantage of others sexually?

How about unselfishness?
Can you name times you have put others before yourself or even equal
    to yourself?
Have there been times you have insisted on your own way?
In relationships do you tend to use others?

Finally, how committed are you to loving God, yourself, and others?
How regularly do you make time for God?
Do you ever want to be the brightest, funniest, prettiest, friendliest, most
    competent, or most charming when you are in a group of people?
What positive and negative examples can you name when it comes to
    loving others?
Do you ever hold on to grudges?
Do you love your enemies or want to strike back at them?
What part have you played in broken relationships?

The "Sermon On The Mount" Approach

Another way to take a moral inventory is to read Jesus's Sermon on the Mount (Matthew 5-7) and list those times you have lived up to the Sermon and those times when you have fallen short. For example, consider Jesus's words on adultery and sexuality:

You have heard that it was said, "You shall not commit adultery." But I say to you that everyone who looks at a woman with lust has already committed adultery with her in his heart. If your right eye causes you to sin, tear it out and throw it away; it is better for you to lose one of your members than for your whole body to be thrown into hell. And if your right hand causes you to sin, cut it off and throw it away; it is better for you to lose one of your members than for your whole body to go into hell. (Matthew 5:27-30)

Your reflections might go something like this:

When have I gone beyond appreciating someone's body to focusing my energy on it?
Have there been times my eyes have led me astray?
Have my hands lashed out in physical force instead of an embrace?

If you choose this approach, work through the entire Sermon. Evaluate yourself on such things as meekness, showing mercy, criticalness, purity, the Golden Rule, peacemaking, anger, greed, boastfulness, and worry. As you read each section of the Sermon, stop, reflect, and write down on paper where you have "stacked up" and "fallen short."

The "Seven Deadly Sins" Approach

Some people use the Seven Deadly Sins as a gauge. The earliest list of the seven is actually in the book of Proverbs:

There are six things that the LORD hates, seven that are an abomination to him: haughty eyes, a lying tongue, and hands that shed innocent blood, a heart that devises wicked plans, feet that hurry to run to evil, a lying witness who testifies falsely, and one who sows discord in a family. (Proverbs 6:16-19)

Around 600 A.D. Gregory the Great suggested that every sin could be traced back to seven "cardinal" or root sins from which all other sins derive, and these (pride, envy, gluttony, lust, anger, greed, sloth) became known as the Seven Deadly Sins. They are called "deadly" because they wound love, and therefore do great harm to our relationship with God and others.

Pride is excessive belief in one's own abilities. Pride says things like, "At least I'm better than . . ." and "I deserve more," or "I don't need God. I can handle this on my own." It has been called the sin from which all others arise. Pride's polar opposite is humility. Where would you place yourself on the Pride-Humility continuum? When have you been prideful? Humble?

Envy is the desire of another's traits, status, abilities, or situation. The envious suffer from chronic dissatisfaction. What do you envy? Do you find it difficult to celebrate another's good fortune? Envy's opposite is contentment. Where would you place yourself on the Envy-Contentment continuum? What examples can you name of both?

Gluttony is an inordinate desire to consume more than we require. It can involve doing anything to excess, be it eating, drinking, exercising, sleeping, or playing. Gluttony's opposite is temperance or moderation. Where are you on the Gluttony-Temperance continuum?

Lust is an inordinate craving for the pleasures of the body. Do you appreciate others or fantasize about others? Do you see people or bodies? Lust's opposite is self-control. Where are you on the Lust-Self-Control continuum? What examples can you give of both?

Anger shows up when we spurn love and opt instead for fury. This deadly sin can also show up as resentment or bitterness. Do you have any ongoing resentments? Are you carrying any grudges? Anger's polar opposite is compassion or gentleness. Where are you on the Anger-Compassion continuum? What specific examples can you give of inappropriate anger? What examples of kindness and compassion can you offer?

Greed is the desire for material wealth or gain. It is a preoccupation with material things. It is also called avarice or covetousness. Greed steals the enjoyment of what we have because we are focused on wanting more. Its opposite is generosity. Where are you on the Greed-Generosity continuum?

Sloth is the avoidance of work or doing the work listlessly. We can be "selective" sloths. We can work hard at making a living but not work hard on knowing how to live. We can work hard at the office but not on our relationships at home. Sloth's opposite is zeal or enthusiasm. Where are you on the Sloth-Zeal continuum?

You have probably heard sermons on the "fullness" of the Holy Spirit, the "comfort" of the Holy Spirit, the "counsel" of the Holy Spirit, and the "baptism" of the Holy Spirit, but not likely on the "searching" of the Spirit. As you take this Fourth Step, ask the Holy Spirit to search you out. Ask the Spirit to give you an honest appraisal of where you are missing the mark and where you are hitting the mark. Do not do self-examination, but rather invite God to examine you. That is all this Fourth Step requires: not to resolve the problems, just to see them.

Summary Points to Ponder

◈ *God is the ultimate "know it all." There is nothing that God does not know about us.*

◈ *How can God's knowledge be wonderful? It is wonderful if the desire of our heart is to please God. If we have taken the Third Step, God knows we want to change. God knows our desire to live differently.*

◈ *"Search me, O God, and know my heart." That's the courageous requirement of Step Four.*

◈ *Because of the deeply personal and radical honesty of the Fourth Step, we need to ask God to protect us and assure us. A belief in a caring God to whom we have surrendered our wills and our lives is essential.*

◈ *"Nothing can separate us from the love of God."*

◈ *Making a moral inventory is not an exercise in character assassination. It is an inventory that includes the good and the not-so-good.*

◈ *The more specific we can be during our inventory, the better.*

◉   *The Fourth Step is not a Step to hurry through.*

◉   *Do not do self-examination but rather invite God to examine you. That is all this Fourth Step requires: not to resolve the problems, just to see them.*

Personal Exercise

1. Meditate on the following passages of Scripture:
   a. Lamentations 3:40
   b. Matthew 23:25-28
   c. Psalm 139
   d. Jeremiah 17:10
   e. 1 Corinthians 2:9-12

2. Choose one of the three approaches (Four Absolutes, Sermon on the Mount, or Seven Deadly Sins) for beginning your moral inventory. Remember, do not rush it. Write your thoughts down on paper and put them in a place where no one but you will read it. Do not forget to include the positive as well as the negative.

Group Sharing and Discussion

1. Where did you "hit the mark" this past week (doing something that put a smile on God's face)? Where did you "miss the mark"?

2. What grabbed your attention in this chapter?

3. What's your "gut" reaction to the Fourth Step?
   a. I do not like to write.
   b. It's pretty scary.
   c. I'm not sure I can handle it.
   d. Will God really protect and assure me through it?
   e. I am not convinced it's really necessary.

f. I like the balance between the good and the bad.

g. Great! I cannot wait to get started.

h. Other.

4. Since the Fourth Step includes the positive as well as the negative, take time in the group to build one another up in love. Hand out blank 3x5 cards to members of the group. If there are eight in the group, give each person seven cards; if ten, give each person nine cards. Ask them to write the name of each group member on a card and then write down a positive quality they see in that person. Give them time to fill out the cards and give the completed cards to the group members. This will help people begin their moral inventory on a positive note.

Chapter 5

Coming Clean

Step Five: We admitted to God, to ourselves, and to another human being the exact nature of our wrongs.

John Westfall is not your typical Presbyterian pastor. Due to his love of eating and cooking Cajun food, he proclaims himself a "hothead." He sometimes plays his "Black Strat" guitar with the worship bands, with the deep and abiding conviction that the guitars can't be loud enough. In his book *Coloring Outside the Lines*, he makes a startling confession:

> At the church I serve, one of my least favorite parts of the worship service is the Prayer of Confession. In most churches the pastor can lead a prepared confession filled with vague generalities about our corporate failure to be all that we can be. But a few years ago at a

staff meeting, it was decided that whoever had that assignment in the worship service should just confess his or her own sin from the previous week. That seemed more authentic and in turn would model genuine confession for the congregation.

One particular Sunday, I was assigned that prayer in the service. It had been a terrible week for me, one in which family tensions had dominated. I wasn't feeling very spiritual, and I was not acting very loving toward my wife, my son, or God. So I did the sensible thing and wrote out a vague, generic, religious-sounding confession to be read in the service.

Sitting in front of the congregation that morning, I felt far from the people, far from my family, far from God, and I was pouting because I felt sorry for myself. My mind was anywhere but on worship as I got up to read my confession. Just then my brain shorted out and I lost my presence of mind, and instead of reading the written prayer I said, "Lord, you know that this has been a terrible week. I have been a jerk at home, and I was so unloving that I put my fist through the bedroom wall while fighting with my wife. I need your forgiveness. Amen." I sat down.

You could have heard a pin drop in the sanctuary. Several things happened that morning. Immediately following the service, three contractors offered their services to replaster my bedroom wall. But more importantly, I was suddenly freed to worship in a fresh way. There were no secrets to hold inside. Everyone knew now that I was not a loving, patient saint of husband and father. I was able to experience the healing that comes when we allow ourselves to be recipients of grace.[17]

The Vertical Dimension

Step Five reads: *We admitted to God, to ourselves, and to another human being the exact nature of our wrongs.* Note the threefold nature of confession: to God, to ourselves, and to another human being. The vertical dimension of confession is our honesty before God. Many of us have heard and experienced the truth of the Apostle John's words: "If we confess our sins, he who is faithful and just will forgive our sins and cleanse us from all unrighteousness" (1 John 1:9). The word "forgive" in the Greek literally means "to leave behind" or "abandon." The Apostle John promises that when we confess our sins to God, God forgives us and, thus, we can leave behind the weight of our wrongdoing. That is great news. We may have expected the opposite. We may have expected God to condemn us rather than forgive us. We may have expected the hammer to fall when we came clean, but just the opposite occurs. We experience grace rather than condemnation.

According to the Scriptures, God's willingness to hear our confession and forgive is limitless. David from the Old Testament, author of many of the great psalms on confession and forgiveness, is a prime example. Though one of the great heroes of the Bible, he was also a greatly flawed individual. Whatever we have done wrong, David likely did in spades, from lying to adultery to having a man killed. How did this flawed individual become such a spiritual hero? He did it through confession. When he could no longer stand the guilt of his sin, he came to God. He came to God repeatedly, and each time he left that encounter feeling lighter in spirit, with the weight of his sin removed.

Listen to the weight he carried:

There is no soundness in my flesh because of your indignation;
there is no health in my bones because of my sin.
For my iniquities have gone over my head;
they weigh like a burden too heavy for me. (Psalm 38:3-4)

David knew, however, where to find relief:

Happy are those whose transgression is forgiven,
whose sin is covered.
Happy are those to whom the Lord imputes not iniquity,
and in whose spirit there is no deceit. (Psalm 32:1-2)

One day I was working on my computer when a warning, highlighted by a big red exclamation point, popped up on my screen. My virus protection program had discovered a virus in an e-mail attachment. The program asked me, "Do you want to remove the virus?" Well, of course,

I did! It wouldn't make any sense to load a virus protection program on a computer and not use it. I clicked "yes," and the program removed the virus. God makes a similar offer: Do we want to be infected, weighed down by our sin and guilt, or do we want to be released from it?

John Bunyan, in his book *Pilgrim's Progress,* spoke to the weight of sin and the freedom that comes from taking our sin to God.

> Now I saw in my dream that the highway up which Christian was to go was fenced on either side with a wall, and that wall is called salvation. Up this way therefore did burdensome Christian run, but not without great difficulty, because of the load on his back. He ran thus till he came at a place somewhat ascending, and upon that place stood a cross, and a little below in the bottom, a sepulchre. So I saw in my dream, that just as Christian came up with the cross, his burden loosed from off his shoulders, and fell from off his back, and began to tumble, and so continued to do, till it came to the mouth of the sepulchre, where it fell in, and I saw it no more.[18]

The Internal Dimension

When we practice the vertical dimension of confession, we understand the joy that springs from forgiveness. We also need to understand the importance of the internal dimension of confession. It is the weight of our sin that pushes us to God. Without facing our sinfulness, we would have no need for God.

A man asked a pastor, "You say that every person carries the weight of sin in his or her life. Well, I feel nothing. How heavy is sin? Is it ten pounds? Eighty pounds? A hundred pounds?

"Let me ask you something," the pastor inquired. "If you laid a four-hundred pound weight on a corpse, would it feel the weight?"

The man replied, "It wouldn't feel anything because it's dead."

The pastor replied, "So it is with people who are spiritually dead. They, too, do not feel the heavy load of sin."

The more alive we become spiritually, the more attuned we become to the error of our ways. Unfortunately, over the years we have been so concerned about building self-esteem, and not saying anything negative, that we've stopped talking about sin. The Scriptures, however, make it clear. We are the apple of God's eye *and* we are incorrigible sinners. Both are true—both are true at the same time—and one without the other corrupts our understanding of who we are. If we downplay our sinfulness, we will have an inflated picture of ourselves. If we overemphasize our sinfulness, we run the risk of denying God's handiwork. As someone once said, "God does not make junk!"

A standardized math test was given to teen-agers from six different nations. In addition to the math questions themselves, the test asked the students to respond "yes" or "no" to the statement, "I am good at mathematics." American students scored lowest on the math questions, far behind the Korean students who had top scores. Ironically, more than three-fourths of the Korean students responded "no" to the "I am good at math" question. In stark contrast, however, sixty-eight percent of the American students believed their math skills were just fine. Our kids may be failing math, but they feel good about themselves!

The American students had a problem: They thought too highly of themselves. They overstated their competency. They were blind to the fact that they had math deficiencies, at least compared to Korean students. Likewise, if we do not come face-to-face with our own deficiencies, we will wander through life with an exaggerated image of who we are. We will go through life unaware of problems that need to be fixed. We will see no need to come to the cross. Admitting our sinfulness pushes us to God, the one who can fix us.

The Horizontal Dimension

We know admitting our sin to ourselves and taking that sin to God renews our strength, but what about the horizontal dimension? Why do we have to tell another human being? Isn't admitting our sin to ourselves and God enough? Why do we have to drag another person into it?

This is where many people balk in the Twelve Step process. They say, "I could never do that. I could never tell another person what I have done, said, and thought. If I did, it would be over between us. They would never look at me the same way again. They would not want to be around me any longer." That, of course, is a valid concern. Given the risk of rejection, why do we have to admit our sins to another human being?

The Bible provides the primary reason. James wrote,

> Therefore confess your sins to one another,
> and pray for one another,
> so that you may be healed. (James 5:16)

This is not the first time Scripture mentions public acknowledgment of sin. We find it in the ancient Mosaic Law: "When a man or a woman wrongs another, breaking faith with the LORD, that person incurs guilt and shall confess the sin that has been committed. The person shall make full restitution for the wrong, adding one fifth to it, and giving it to the one who was wronged" (Numbers 5:6-7). James, however, took this horizontal dimension of confession a step further. He went beyond merely coming clean to the person we have harmed (as important as that may be). He went all the way to linking confession to our healing—emotional, relational, physical, mental, and spiritual. According to James, horizontal confession is a key to becoming whole persons. James believed deeply, not only in Christ, but also in the healing power of openness.

As a pastor, I have been blessed by people sharing their joys, struggles, hopes, fears, and failures with me. I have even been especially privileged to hear some people's Fifth Step. Each time I've listened, an interesting thing has happened: Instead of being repulsed, I've been impressed. These people have so much courage. They have such a desire to grow in Christ. At times, after listening to their stories, I've thought to myself, "This person is more spiritual than I am, and I'm his or her pastor!" Most times when people finish sharing their Fifth Step, they breathe a sigh of relief, we hug, and we share a special bond from that day forward. Moreover, most of them point back to sharing their Fifth Step as a watershed moment in their lives. From that time on, they become more authentic individuals. They no longer feel a need to protect their image. They feel free to be the person God created them to be.

Charles Swindoll made a wise observation in his book *The Quest for Character:*

From a distance we're all beautiful people. Well-dressed, nice smile, friendly looking, cultured, under control, at peace. But what a different picture when someone comes up close and gets in touch! What appeared so placid is really a mixture: winding roads of insecurity and uncertainty, maddening gusts of lust, greed, self-indulgence, pathways of pride glazed over with a slick layer of hypocrisy; all this shrouded in a cloud of fear of being found out. From a distance we dazzle . . . up close we are tarnished. Put enough of us together and we may resemble an impressive mountain range. But when you get down into the shadowy crevices . . . the Alps we ain't.[19]

That's the human condition. We each have chinks in our armor, flaws we attempt to keep under wraps. We are not strange or odd by any means. We are merely human. Living an illusion—weaving lies, putting on airs, hiding the truth about ourselves—takes great energy. If we want to become whole, we need to stop pretending we are different from the rest of the human race. We no longer need to exert energy maintaining an illusion of who we are. When we come out of the shadows and into the light, we will find others like us—and relief from the stress of pretending.

The truth is, we can grow only so far alone, and then we reach a point where continued growth requires help from someone else. In Step Five we reach that point. If we have completed the moral inventory in Step Four, we may not be feeling very good about ourselves. Yes, we listed our positive attitudes, traits, and behaviors, but we also listed a bunch of stuff we have been hiding from others. We may not feel very lovable. We may want to abort the process. We may not want to go any further. We may feel particularly vulnerable. At this point we need someone to come alongside of us to incarnate God's grace to us.

I like the story of the little boy, who after being tucked into bed for the night, cried out, "Mommy, I'm afraid to be alone in the dark. I want somebody to stay with me."

His mother responded, "Don't be afraid. God is with you."

The little boy said sadly, "I want somebody with skin on his face."

After completing the Fourth Step, we need somebody with skin on his or her face to say to us, "By the grace of God you are forgiven. God loves you, and so do I." Listen to how the great reformer Martin Luther put it in *A Prelude on Babylonian Captivity of the Church*:

> It [confession] is useful, even necessary. I would not have it abolished. Indeed I rejoice that it exists in the Church of Christ, for it is a cure without equal for distressed consciences. For when we have laid bare our conscience to a brother or sister and privately made known to that person the evil that lurked within, we receive from his or her lips the word of comfort spoken by God.[20]

That has been my experience. I made a mistake recently and asked a good friend to listen to me for a few minutes. During that "five-minute mini–Fifth Step," an interesting thing happened. His eyes, his demeanor, his nods of understanding, his compassion reacquainted me with the fact that God is a gracious God who understands the human condition. That gets blurry for me from time to time. After all, I am a "professional" Christian. I have been a pastor. I have preached in pulpits. I have spoken at conferences. I have lead retreats. I have consciously walked with God since the summer of 1975, but when I stumble, I get so disappointed in myself. I feel like a terrible person, a real hypocrite who does not practice what he preaches. Then I take a mini–Fifth Step and tell a trusted friend, and my friend becomes a reflection of God. My friend becomes Jesus with skin on his face. That's the power of confessing to another human being.

Choosing a Confessor

A cartoon shows a pastor sitting at this desk working a hand puppet. The caption reads, "Rev. Roadcup finally finds a friend to whom he can bear his soul."[21] At this point we need to ask, "Who can I trust to hear my Fifth Step?" It's an important decision because the wrong person could do us harm. In addition, the power of openness can be invigorating. Having told one person and received God's grace, we are tempted to tell everyone. We need to be careful. Not everyone can be trusted. Some may use the information to hurt us. And some people we may downright scare! They are not accustomed to such transparency. If we tell the right person, however, it can be transformational. So, to whom should we turn to hear our Fifth Step?

People usually choose someone whom they consider trustworthy, compassionate, and a good listener. They then set up a meeting with this person to share all they have learned about themselves from the Fourth Step. They share with this person their character defects, their specific sins, and controlling behaviors. After sharing, they listen to any feedback the listener has for them. In choosing a suitable confessor, consider the following qualities.

Choose someone who keeps confidences. The person we choose needs to be someone who has a proven track record when it comes to keeping confidences. We do not want any of the information we share leaking out to others. We want to be assured that what we share will stay just between the two of us.

Kenneth Quick coined a clever little phrase when it comes to confidentiality. When we have a secret to tell, we want to make sure people will keep what we say to them in strictest confidence. So we make overtures to people, wondering, asking, and probing if they can keep what we say to themselves. We ask things such as, "Are you sure you won't share this with anyone?" or "Can I trust you to keep this to yourself?" or "Do you cross your heart and hope to die that what I tell you will never pass your lips?" He calls these overtures " 'Will You Tell?' Overtures."[22]

The older I get, the fewer people I know who can be trusted with confidential information. Keeping confidences appears to be a rare, and much needed, trait. The physician's Hippocratic Oath comes to mind:

> And whatsoever I shall see or hear in the course of my profession . . . if it be what should not be published abroad, I will never divulge, holding such things to be holy secrets.

The same applies to hearers of our Fifth Step. The confidences we share with another are holy secrets, to be guarded as closely as that of a doctor-patient or attorney-client relationship.

Choose someone dedicated to spiritual growth themselves. Whomever we choose needs to appreciate the value of what we are doing. They need to understand the significance of sin, confession, and forgiveness, and feel honored to be asked to participate in such an important spiritual moment. They need to operate by the principle, "To err is human, to admit is superhuman!" They need to comprehend the courageousness of our act, to recognize that not everyone has the guts to do this. They also need to be mature enough to reflect back God's mercy and grace. This person needs to be able to assure us that we should never be ashamed to say what we have done wrong, since what we are really doing is simply admitting we are wiser today than we were yesterday. This person might be a priest, pastor, counselor, mentor, spiritual director, or friend. Some, wanting to guard their anonymity, may want to go out of town to find such a person. In town, or out of town, we need to find someone on a spiritual journey themselves.

Choose someone who is street-smart. We also want someone acquainted enough with the ways of humanity that they won't be blown away by whatever we confess. A Roman Catholic priest once described the experience of hearing the confession of nuns "like being stoned to death with popcorn." But most of us will be flinging more than popcorn, and we need someone who can handle it. As we work through issues such as gluttony, pride, lust, greed, sexuality, anger, and selfishness, our confessor needs to be able to withstand the muck and mire we toss their way. We do not want someone who will stare at us in shock, eyes wide open. They do not need to have been around the block themselves, but they need to know the types of things around the block.

They also need to be smart enough to keep us from shifting the focus. Working through the Fifth Step is not a license to destroy other people. This is not a "tell-all, name-names exposé." Exposing other people's sin is not the purpose of the Fifth Step. If we begin to name someone with whom we were involved in sinful ways, a good listener will stop us in our tracks. Other people's names are not important. Their part in the immorality is not important. Our part is. We need to find someone who makes sure we do our Fifth Step and not someone else's.

The Proper Response to God's Grace, Mercy, and Forgiveness

Few experiences in life are more humbling than admitting to God, ourselves, and another human being the exact nature of our wrongs. Yet, few experiences are more necessary for long-term peace of mind, healing, and wholeness than this significant Step.

On a Christmas Eve, worshipers arrived at Central Presbyterian Church in Atlanta for the 9:00 PM service. They had to push through a crowd of roughly fifty homeless men who had gathered outside the church. Central's homeless shelter was full, and the men were waiting for a bus that would transport them to another shelter. When nine o'clock arrived, the choir and clergy processed into the sanctuary. The congregation joined together in a corporate prayer of confession, and the liturgist offered the assurance of pardon, "Friends, hear and believe the good news of the Gospel! In Jesus Christ we are forgiven!" At that exact moment something startling happened. A huge cheer went up outside the church. The waiting men were cheering because the bus had arrived. The pastor and those parishioners will never again hear the words of forgiveness, cleansing, and renewal without remembering that the proper response to God's grace, mercy, and forgiveness is "Hooray!"

That's what Step Five offers us: We receive God's forgiveness and cleansing. We see the compassionate face of Christ working through a trusted friend, counselor, pastor, mentor, priest, or confidante. Hooray!

Summary Points to Ponder

- *Step Five embraces three levels of confession: to God, to ourselves, and to another human being.*

- *God's willingness to hear our confession and forgive is limitless.*

- *The weight of our sin pushes us to God. Without facing our sinfulness, we would have no need for God.*

@ *The more alive we become spiritually, the more attuned we become to the error of our ways.*

@ *The truth is, we can grow only so far alone, and then we reach a point where continued growth requires help from someone else.*

@ *If we want to become whole, we need to stop pretending we are different from the rest of the human race. We no longer need to exert energy maintaining an illusion of who we are.*

@ *We need someone to come alongside of us to incarnate God's grace to us.*

@ *The person we choose to hear our confession needs to be someone who has a proven track record when it comes to keeping confidences.*

@ *Whomever we choose needs to appreciate the value of what we are doing. They need to understand the significance of sin, confession, and forgiveness, and feel honored to be asked to participate in such an important spiritual moment.*

@ *We want someone acquainted enough with the ways of humanity so as not to be blown away by whatever we confess.*

Personal Exercises

1. Read through and meditate on:
    a. Psalm 32:3-5
    b. 1 John 1:5-2:2
    c. James 5:16
    d. Proverbs 28:13

2. Begin confessing the exact nature of your wrongs to God. Do not hurry through it. You may want to take ten minutes a day for the

next couple of weeks. Take note of how you are feeling as you go through this process with God.

3. Make a list of a handful of people you think fit the criteria for someone to hear your Fifth Step. Pray about the names on the list. Which person or persons does God seem to lift from your list?

Group Sharing and Discussion

1. How would you describe your childhood home environment?
   a. Everyone towed the line.
   b. Open and honest.
   c. Understanding and compassionate.
   d. Kept secrets.
   e. Fault finding.
   f. Encouraging.
   g. Warm and loving.
   h. Unforgiving.
   i. Other.

2. What piqued your interest from this chapter?

3. What pops into your mind about choosing someone to hear your Fifth Step?
   a. No way.
   b. I'll have to think about it.
   c. No one comes to mind.
   d. Do I really have to do it?
   e. I've already asked someone to hear it.
   f. I'm raring to go.
   g. I have been doing something similar for a while.
   h. I cannot think of doing anything much scarier.
   i. Other.

Chapter 6

Get Ready, Get Set, Go

Step Six: We were entirely ready to have God remove all these defects of character.

Step Seven: We humbly asked [God] to remove all our shortcomings.

One of my desires is to attend a major league baseball game in every major league city. I also want to collect as many baseball movies on DVD as possible. My family has given them to me for birthdays, Christmas, Father's Day, and I have purchased some myself . . . *Field of Dreams, For the Love of the Game, Pride of the Yankees, The Sandlot, Bull Durham,* and *The Natural.*

One baseball movie on my wish list is the 1992 box office bust *Mr. Baseball.* It is the story of Jack Elliot, an aging power hitter who was traded to a Japanese team. His new team, the Chiunichi Dragons, expected him to power them to a pennant. Jack got off to a hot start, and everyone loved him. The Japanese press gave him the nickname "Mr. Baseball." Then he cooled off at the plate. He became an "easy" out. His life began to fall apart. He had trouble adjusting to Japanese customs. He resisted what he considered ridiculous and arbitrary rules of the club and belittled the etiquette expected of him as a representative of his team. To complicate matters, the Japanese manager, whom Jack despised, noticed a "hole" in Jack's swing. Jack, however, did not see the flaw. He was too busy blaming other people for his difficulties to notice the problem. After falling in love with his translator, the manager's daughter, he began to rethink his attitude. He faced his problem and was finally ready to make the necessary changes. And in humility, he eventually realized he needed the manager's help in fixing it.

That's what the next two Steps are about, readiness and humility. Step Six reads: *We were entirely ready to have God remove all our defects of character.* Step Seven reads: *We humbly asked [God] to remove all our shortcomings.* These two Steps challenge us. These two Steps ask us to give up behaviors that have long dominated our lives. We know how harmful these behaviors have been to us and others; still, they have been a part of us for as long as we can remember. These Steps may not be easy. They may take awhile. But they are the stepping stones to ongoing spiritual renewal.

Step Six

The Sixth Step asks us to assess our "readiness" factor. Are we entirely ready to have God remove all our defects of character? Are we entirely ready to allow God to fix the "hole" in our swing? Are we entirely ready to stop blaming others for our problem? Are we entirely ready to stop thinking we can fix ourselves? Are we entirely ready to avail ourselves of God's power and input? Are we entirely ready to allow God's power to be released within us, to flow through us and cleanse us? Are we entirely ready to give up control? Are we entirely ready for God to remove our character defects as God—not we—sees fit? Our readiness quotient is the doorway to active and effective change of lifelong habits and compulsions.

A Critical Question

In the fifth chapter of his Gospel, John recounted Jesus's encounter with a crippled man by the Pool of Bethesda, a pool reputed to have healing powers. When the surface of the water started stirring, everyone headed for the pool. For thirty-eight years this man had been waiting for someone to lower him into the water. When Jesus saw him, Jesus asked what seems to be a rhetorical question: "Do you want to be made well?" Well, of course, he did. He'd been waiting there for thirty-eight years! This guy had committed his life to getting well.

But hold on a moment. What if Jesus's question was not rhetorical? What if Jesus did not assume the answer? Some people, after all, become comfortable with their afflictions. They build their lives around their problems. Maybe this guy liked his problem. Maybe he liked blaming others for his condition. He certainly blamed others when he responded to Jesus: "Sir, I have no one to put me into the pool when the water is stirred up; and while I am making my way, someone else steps down ahead of me" (John 5:7). In other words, "If others were more thoughtful and less pushy, I would have been in that water. Do you think hanging around here is a bed of roses? It's not. My butt's flat from lying on this hard ground, and you ask me, 'Do you want to be made well?' What kind of stupid question is that?"

The man's response was not an answer to Jesus's question. The man gave a reason why he had been there so long, but he did not reveal his "readiness quotient." So Jesus tested the invalid's state of mind: "Stand up, take your mat, and walk." The rubber suddenly met the road. What would the cripple do? Would he blame others? Would he be cynical: "Are you nuts, Jesus? Didn't I just tell you I can't walk? How could I possibly stand and walk?" Would he hold onto his known way of existing? After all, the regulars at the pool knew him. As in the television sitcom *Cheers*, everybody likely knew his name. Being crippled meant he didn't have to take on many responsibilities. He didn't have to work. If he took up Jesus's directive to, "Stand up and walk," it would be a whole new way of life. He could no longer wallow in self-pity. The man had to respond. He had to do something. When push came to shove, would he attempt to get on his feet? Was he "entirely ready"?

A Sincere Assessment

That's how it is with our lifelong character defects. As painful and destructive as they are, we know them. We have had them for a long time. They are like an old pair of jeans: ragged and worn, but familiar, maybe even a little comfortable . . . like my pessimism. I've been a pessimist as long as I can remember. My pessimism frustrates my wife, a born optimist. Thankfully, I'm loveable in many other ways, but this is not one of them. I do not like to get my hopes up because they may get dashed. I do not allow myself to get too excited until I know something for certain will happen. My knee-jerk reaction is to expect the worst. I say things to myself such as, "No way they will pick me," or "Don't get your hopes up. The chances of this coming together are slim," or "This is not going to work."

For fifty-plus years this character defect has served me well. Sure, I'm not all that joyful. Sure, I reign myself in. Sure, I protect myself so I won't get hurt and disappointed. Sure, most of the bad things I think might happen never do. Sure, I constantly look for upcoming storms. Sure, I drive my optimistic wife nuts. But what happens if I become an optimist and something bad happens? Won't that destroy me? Won't that catch me so off guard that I may not recover? Being a pessimist has its advantages. It helps me assess the downside of every venture, every opportunity, and every risk. It helps me anticipate approaching disaster. I am great at evaluating all the things that could go wrong. Take the first cruise we planned. I thought of all the ways we could miss the cruise ship: flat tire on the way to the airport, airline strike, computer glitch, lost tickets, airline bankruptcy, mechanical problem on plane, missed connection, bad weather, terrorist attack, oversleep, SARS epidemic, heart attack, stroke, family death. I told Trudy, "I am not going to let myself get excited about the cruise until we get on the ship. Too many things could go wrong." What would it be like to get rid of those old, worn, and ragged pessimist jeans? Would I be comfortable in a different pair of jeans? Like the crippled man at the Bethesda, I need to answer the question, "Do I *really* want to be made well?"

Do we really want to be freed from pride? Isn't it fun to feel superior to others? Do we really want to stop raging? Isn't the adrenaline rush of flying off the handle and watching people cower in our presence invigorating? Do we really want to stop lusting? We surely would miss those sexual fantasies. Do we really want to be less gluttonous? Doesn't it feel good to feed our emotions? Do we really want to abandon our greed? We like the things we have purchased. Do we really want to ditch envy? We do, after all, deserve more. Do we really want to discard self-ishness? Who would watch out for us if we did? Do we really want to be less controlling? What if others don't get it or don't do it right? Do we really want to get rid of perfectionism? We enjoy the praise it brings our way. Do we really want to stop lying? People probably would not like us as much if we told the truth about ourselves.

Also, if we abandon so much of ourselves, who's going to be left? Who will we be if we discard much of whom we have been? Will we be like the patient being discharged from a mental institution? As the patient walked out, the doctor proudly proclaimed, "You are cured." "Some cure," the man replied. "When I first came here, I was Abraham Lincoln. Now, I'm nobody."

Who will we be after we allow these changes to be made? Do we *really* want to be made well? Are we really ready to have God remove these character defects from us? Intellectually, we may be. Intellectu-ally, we may be saying, "Yes. I've had it with these defects. I'm ready for a change. I'm ready to stand, pick up my mat, and move to a new place." Emotionally, however, may be another matter.

To take this Sixth Step, we say, "That's it. I'm ready for a significant change. Yes, these character defects give me a sense of pleasure, as warped as that may be, and yes, these defects are comfortable like a pair of old jeans. But the cost of keeping them is too high. I'm ready now to release them to God."

Step Seven

If Step Six is the "get ready" Step, Step Seven is the "go" Step. In Step Six we got ready for God to remove our character defects. In Step Seven we humbly ask God to remove them.

Humility—that's a challenge. We are not naturally humble. We are by nature, or nurture, demanding. We demand that our spouses respond to our needs. We demand to be heard. We demand that our churches be sensitive to our concerns. We demand our rights. We demand slow drivers to move out of the passing lane. We demand a refund. We demand that legitimate pleasures be ours to enjoy. Laura Beth Jones captures our spirit in *Jesus in Blue Jeans*:

> It is not surprising that the portion of the federal budget that is threatening to bankrupt our country is called "entitlements." Sometime after World War II, we as a society, got the idea that the government was supposed to take care of us from the cradle to the grave, and we have all been paying for the notion ever since. We also are often called "ugly Americans" overseas because of an attitude that, because we are Americans, things should be done for us in a certain way, in a certain manner, and darn quickly, thank you.[23]

Of course, being humility-challenged is nothing new. The ancient Israelites required a number of years to learn it. Moses reminded them, "Remember the long way that the LORD your God has led you these forty years in the wilderness, in order to humble you, testing you to know what was in your heart, whether or not you would keep his commandments" (Deuteronomy 8:2). If it takes us that long to learn humility, we may never get to it.

I love the story of the grandfather who proudly took his granddaughter to work. He put her on his shoulders and paraded her around the office, introducing her to co-workers. His boss, who had met her before, said to her with a twinkle in his eye, "My goodness, how you've grown! You are about three times as big as you were last year."

The little girl replied, "Not all of this is me."

No matter who we are, no matter our accomplishments or standing in life, all of us are riding on the shoulders of people who have helped and encouraged us. Most of all, we are riding on the shoulders of God.

Humility has nothing to do with putting ourselves down. It does not equal low self-esteem. Humility, rather, has to do with understanding our place before God. Humility understands how much we need God. Humility appreciates the immensity of God's power to transform lives. Humility says along with the prophet Zechariah, "Not by might, nor by power, but by my spirit, says the LORD of hosts" (Zechariah 4:6).

Most of us have not been taught humility. We have been taught the opposite. We have worked hard on building self-esteem and a solid self-reliance that declares, "I can do it on my own." We have developed an all-American way of rugged individualism in contrast to humility before God. There is nothing wrong with self-esteem, or the ability to conquer something on our own, or the sense of adventure that leads us to reach beyond ourselves. It's the manner in which we do these things that makes them wrong: a manner that embraces too much self and not enough others, and most specifically not enough God. When we neglect to come humbly into the presence of the Author of all things, seeking guidance and strength, we are declaring, "I know what is best for me. I do not have time for you." We become self-reliant and exaggerate our own strength and ability. We resemble the Pharisee who strolled into prayer expounding his goodness: God was certainly fortunate to have him on the team. The tax collector, on the other hand, knowing his proper state before God, pleaded for forgiveness. He acknowledged a supreme and loving God who could remove his shortcomings and character defects (Luke 18:10-13). The tax collector humbly took Step Seven.

Making Time to Ask

Humility challenges us, but so does asking God to help us. We've discussed some of the questions and concerns about "asking prayer" in chapter 2: What if God says no? What about the times it seems God has let us down? Asking prayer seems so selfish. It's embarrassing to have to ask for anything from anyone. But there are a couple other challenges when it comes to asking prayer.

First, there is the issue of foreign territory. When asking something of God, we enter into a sacred communication with an all-knowing, always present Being, and many of us do not regularly enter this world. Statistics show that, while Americans believe in prayer, we don't spend a lot of time doing it. On the average, a person who strongly asserts herself as a Christian will spend one or two minutes a day in prayer. A pastor, priest, or rabbi will spend eight or ten minutes a day in prayer. For many of us, prayer has been relegated to a mealtime blessing, or a series of quick, "Help me out here, God," requests throughout the day.

Prayer is not our natural habitat. Step Seven, therefore, asks us to do something many of us do not know how to do, or at least do not do very well. It's like entering a foreign land. How do we learn the language of prayer? How do we converse with God? How do we listen to God?

Second, prayer requires something we do not have in abundance: time. Time is the currency of our day. It's a precious commodity. God says to us, "Be still, and know that I am God" (Psalm 46:10). How do we pull that off? Our world is full of distractions, demands, interruptions, and noise. Ironically enough, we have developed numerous "time savers," yet we find ourselves with less time. We can microwave a meal in seconds; send documents in the length of time it takes a phone to ring; instant message one another; transport ourselves across the Atlantic in a few hours and, yet, where does the time go? Instead of saving us time, these advances have only speeded up the pace of our lives.

A man attended an event focused on prayer. When he arrived, he discovered there were no keynote speakers, no workshops, no seminars. The schedule read:

7:30-8:30	Breakfast
8:30-12:00	Prayer
12:00-1:00	Lunch
1:00-6:00	Prayer
6:00-7:00	Dinner
7:00-10:00	Prayer

He said to himself, "This is ridiculous!" But by the end of the first day and into the second, he began experiencing the transforming power of prayer. He realized the necessity to be still before God.

To humbly ask God, we may have to enter foreign territory. We may have to learn a new language. We may have to make time to pray. But communing with God is worth it. When we pray, we develop a relationship with the One who called us into existence. When we pray, we build a relationship with the One who is able to release us from the chains that bear down heavily upon our souls.

Working Step Seven

When we are ready to humbly ask God to remove our shortcomings, we can pray the prayer of the Seventh Step:

> My Creator, I am now willing that you should have all of me, good and bad. I pray that you now remove from me every single defect of character which stands in the way of my usefulness to you and my fellows. Grant me strength, as I go out from here, to do your bidding. Amen.[24]

It's short, but significant. In addition to reciting this prayer, however, we need to keep certain things in mind.

First, we need to remember that this is a birthing process. As such, this Step involves pain. With the pain, however, comes great gain. Jesus said unless we are born of water and of the Spirit, we cannot enter the Kingdom of God (John 3:5). The birth of flesh is human in origin, temporal in nature, and has a beginning and an end. The birth that involves the Spirit of God is of divine origin and is eternal in nature. This birth is not something we can accomplish in our own strength or by our own human power or intelligence.

Second, we need to be specific concerning the character defects we want removed. General prayers often lead to general answers. Specific prayers lead to specific answers. The more specific we can be concerning the character defects we want God to remove, the more aware we will be of the removal. It's a little like the situation in our house. Once a week someone comes to clean, and Trudy leaves a specific list of things, in addition to the usual, that she wants done: dust the master bedroom blinds, mop the entry, and put the clothes in the dryer. When we ask God to clean our house, we also make a list. "God, as you clean my house, please give special attention to my impatience, greed, lying, lust, and anger. I need considerable cleaning up in those areas." This focuses our attention on how the cleaning process is coming along in those specific areas.

Third, we need to recognize that we will never be free from sin and temptation. Four men were sharing their sins with one another in the presence of a priest. One of the men cried out, "How can God let us live on the earth? Why doesn't he kill us to purify creation?"

"Because," the priest answered, "God is a potter; God works in mud."

We are who we are. We will never be sinless. We will never stop being drawn to inappropriate thoughts, actions, and attitudes. We will continue to face the temptation of returning to our old ways. We will never be completely free from our "sin-disease." We will keep seeing character defects that need changing. We will, however, be continually renewed if we humbly, and continually, ask God to create something new and beautiful out of the mud.

Fourth, we need to focus our prayers on bite-sized periods of time. When we lived in Florida, we had a swimming pool heated by solar panels, and we had problems from the get-go. A pipe would break, and we would have water draining off our roof and out of our pool. The first time it happened was scary. We feared the pool's pump might burn out. The second time it happened was a little confusing. Why did this happen again? I thought the problem was fixed. The third time it happened was downright frustrating. After a solar pipe broke for a fourth time, I was ticked.

Remember that I am a giant people-pleaser. I want everyone to like me, even my incompetent solar guy. So here's what I did. I didn't ask God to remove my people-pleasing flaw forever, just for a manageable chunk of time. I prayed, "Lord, I have to call the dealer about the solar heating system. The call is at nine in the morning. Take away this people-pleasing defect in me for just ten minutes. Let me share my anger and frustration during that call. Assure me that the sun will come up tomorrow if someone thinks I am a jerk."

Most of us will be much more successful in asking God to remove our character defects if we can break down our requests into a small, manageable period of time. If we have a problem with over-eating, we can pray, "Lord, only one helping tonight and no dessert. Would you help me just get through tonight?" If we have a problem with anger, we can pray, "Lord, I have a conflict resolution meeting at church tonight. It's from seven to nine. Help me get through it. Help me not to fly off the handle." If we have a problem with spending, we can pray, "Lord, I do not want to use my credit card today. Do not let me charge anything today. It's cash and cash only. Thanks for the help." We don't pray to stop over-eating forever, or raging forever, or over-spending forever. Instead, we take what has been a lifelong problem for us and break it down into something we can work on—for an hour, for a morning, for a day.

Fifth, we need to trust that God will remove our shortcomings in God's own way, in God's own time. Extreme makeovers are in. Of the 6.6 million cosmetic-plastic-surgery patients in 2002, nearly a third had multiple procedures at the same time. In our town a one-stop beauty shop has opened where interested customers can consult with a "concierge" and choose from a menu of services. Total makeovers include cosmetic dentistry, Botox injections, and other cosmetic enhancements. The average cost runs about $20,000. They do not take long and are only skin deep.

We are asking God for something more significant. We want God to perform an extreme takeover and makeover of our inner being. We desire a more beautiful inside. How does God do it? How does God remove our character defects and turn us into more beautiful people? For some, it happens instantly. They no longer have a desire to over-drink, or over-eat, or over-spend. They experience, in effect, a miracle makeover. In a twinkling of an eye, they are a new creation. The old is gone and the new has come. For most of us, however, God deals with our shortcomings slowly, over time. One day we may realize that a certain character defect has diminished power over us. It's still there, and we have to reaffirm daily that we will not return to it, but it's not nearly as difficult to control as it once was. We cannot speed up the process. We cannot force it or manipulate it. All we can do is open ourselves to God. However God removes a character defect—instantly or gradually—the experience is incredible. God makes all things beautiful, in God's time.

Sixth, we need to act in accordance with the changes God is making in our lives. Sanctification is the theological term for an extreme spiritual makeover. It is growing into holiness or wholeness; it's becoming more Christ-like. There are three schools of thought as to how it works.

The first school teaches that God does everything. We pray, "Oh, God take away my character defects. Transform me," and then we put our feet up on the desk and wait for God to do what God will do. The second school teaches just the opposite: "God saved us and then said to us, 'You are on your own. Do your best to work out those changes in your life.'" Then there is the third school of thought. It's the middle ground and the most theologically sound. St. Augustine sums up this school of thought quite well: Pray like it all depends on God. Work like it all depends on you.

As we work the Seventh Step, our actions need to be in harmony with the changes God is making in us. For example, if we have a problem with over-eating, we stop going to buffet restaurants. If we have a problem with over-spending, we take our credit cards out of our wallet. If we have a problem with over-working, we leave the office promptly at five. If we have a problem with pride, we search for good qualities in others. If we have a problem with lust, we steer clear of certain books, magazines, and movies. If we have a problem with our temper, we count to ten or twenty or thirty or one hundred prior to opening our mouths.

Seventh, we need to surround ourselves with friends who know us and our defects and want to see us grow. Just as God told Adam, "It is not good for you to be alone," it is not good for us either.

In Tolkien's *The Fellowship of the Ring,* Frodo was a very courageous hobbit. But he did not stand a chance without Sam, Gandalf, Strider, Gimli, Legolas, Merry, and Pippin. Evil hunted Frodo and a fellowship formed to protect him. Frodo would meet unknown dangers along the way: the mines of Moria, evil orcs, magic spells, searching eyes, the crazed Gollum. He would need friends to look out for him, friends who had his best interests at heart. We need friends like that as well. We need people who will stand with us and lift us up. We need what my friend Stan Ott calls a "Fellowship of the Heart." We need a group of people who will fight for us, support us, and stick with us. The changes we want are life changing. We must not embark on them alone. Only with our friends' support and encouragement will we be equipped to tackle our emotional and behavioral "orcs" and "magic spells."

Ready? Set? Go!

Summary Points to Ponder

⊚ *Steps Six and Seven ask us to give up behaviors that have long domi-nated our lives. These Steps may not be easy. They may take awhile. But they are the stepping stones to ongoing spiritual renewal.*

- As painful and destructive as our lifelong character defects are, we know them. We have had them for a long time. They are like an old pair of jeans: ragged and worn, but familiar, maybe even a little comfortable.

- Step Six asks us to assess our "readiness" factor. "Do you want to be made well?"

- Humility—that's a challenge. We are not naturally humble. We are by nature, or nurture, demanding.

- Humility has nothing to do with putting ourselves down. It does not equal low self-esteem. Humility, rather, has to do with understanding our place before God. Humility understands how much we need God.

- When asking something of God, we enter into a sacred communication with an omnipresent, omniscient Being. We may have to learn a new language. We may have to make time to pray. But communing with God is worth it.

- Step Seven is a birthing process. It is not something we can accomplish in our own strength or by our own human power or intelligence.

- "God is a potter; God works in mud."

- We need a "Fellowship of the Heart"—a group of people who will fight for us, support us, and stick with us.

Personal Exercises

1. Reflect and meditate on the following passages of Scripture:
   a. 2 Corinthians 5:17
   b. John 3:3-6

    c. John 5:2-9

    d. Psalm 103:1-12

    e. Colossians 3:5-10

2. List the specific character defects you want God to remove.

rage, jealousy, Over- working co-dependence

3. Assess your "readiness quotient." Is it:

    a. high?

    b. low?

    c. moderate?

    d. miniscule?

Group Sharing and Discussion

1. Share a time this past week when you felt, "ready and raring to go." Maybe it was a project at work. Maybe it was cleaning out a closet. Maybe it was planning or taking a vacation. Maybe it was sending the kids off somewhere. Maybe it was reading a new book. Maybe it was a game of golf.

2. What spoke personally to you from this chapter? How so?

3. Share one character defect that you would like God to remove from you.

4. How are you doing thus far in working through the Twelve Steps?

    a. I'm feeling out of control.

    b. I'm in a lot of pain.

    c. I'm making progress, slow but sure.

    d. I'm disappointed in myself.

    e. This stuff scares me to death.

    f. This may be the most courageous thing I've ever attempted.

    g. I'm a Step or two behind.

    h. I can't wait for the next Step.

    i. Other.

Section Three

The Make Up Steps

Wherever two or three are gathered in Jesus's name . . . there is conflict! Misunderstandings, clashes, and disagreements are part of the human condition. We have blind spots. We do not always see things clearly. We come from different backgrounds and bring different life experiences to our relationships. We hold a wide range of ideas, thoughts, and feelings. We do not always hear what others say or intend to say. We say and do things we later regret. We hurt and disappoint others inadvertently—and sometimes on purpose. Sometimes we do not even know we have hurt another. Sometimes others do not know we have wronged them. We do things secretly, behind their backs, out of sight. Some relationships withstand the conflicts and disappointments; some do not.

Steps Eight and Nine focus on people we have injured or upset, even if those folk are unaware that we had wronged them. These Steps ask us to acknowledge our responsibility in a broken relationship, and if possible, make amends. The Apostle Paul wrote, "If it is possible, so far as it depends on you, live peaceably with all" (Romans 12:18). In these Steps we become peacemakers. We do not allow the past to stay in the past. Instead, we ask others to forgive the ways in which we have hurt them, and if necessary, we make reparation to them. Some say these two Steps are the most difficult and the most rewarding of all. I agree, at least when it comes to the difficulty of it. It's no fun eating humble pie, but it's another step on the road to spiritual wholeness.

Step Eight: We made a list of all persons we had harmed, and became willing to make amends to them all.

Step Nine: We made direct amends to such people wherever possible, except when to do so would injure them or others.

Chapter 7

Eating
Humble Pie

Step Eight: We made a list of all persons we had harmed, and became willing to make amends to them all.

Step Nine: We made direct amends to such people wherever possible, except when to do so would injure them or others.

On Sunday, June 13, 2004, Matt Starr was at Ameriquest Field in Arlington, Texas, watching the home team Rangers take on the St. Louis Cardinals. When a foul ball was hit toward where he was sitting, the twenty-eight-year-old landscaper leapt over the seat in front of him. Even though the ball had landed at the feet of four-year-old Nicholas O'Brien, Starr knocked the boy against the seats and pounced on the ball. The boy's mother, insulted by the aggressive behavior, swatted him with her program, while fans chanted, "Give the boy the ball." But, clutching the ball to himself, Starr returned to his seat unwilling to part with his new souvenir.

Even the ballplayers witnessed Starr's actions. Between innings, Cardinals' outfielder, Reggie Sanders, went into the stands to give the boy a bat. Nicholas also received souvenirs from the Texas Rangers, including one signed by Hall of Fame pitcher Nolan Ryan. Video of Starr's self-serving behavior was shown on television stations across the country.

When interviewed on "Good Morning America," Nicholas's mother admitted calling Starr a jerk, among other names. "I said, 'You trampled a four-year-old boy to get this ball,' and he said, 'Oh, well.'"

Four days later, Starr, a former youth minister at a nearby church, expressed sorrow for his behavior. He agreed to send a letter of apology to the O'Brien family. Starr also indicated he would give the boy the ball. In addition, he would buy tickets for the entire family to a future Rangers' game.

Most of us have done something just as insensitive, but thankfully not before a national television audience. We have trampled over someone's feelings, but never have we been invited on *Good Morning America, The Tonight Show,* or ESPN to explain our behavior. In all likelihood more than one person feels toward us as little Nicholas O'Brien felt toward Matt Starr. When we treat people poorly, they remember it. They remember it well, and so do we. We still cringe when we think about how selfishly and insensitively we have acted. The memory of it still haunts us.

The Make Up Steps and the Bible

Steps Eight and Nine are "reconciliation" Steps or "restitution" Steps. They ask us to make a list of people we have injured, attempt to heal the relationship, and make amends wherever possible.

Step Eight reads: *We made a list of all persons we had harmed, and became willing to make amends to them all.*

Step Nine reads: *We made direct amends to such people wherever possible, except when to do so would injure them or others.*

Where did the authors of these Steps come up with them? They got them from the Bible. Two primary passages come to mind. The first is the story of Zacchaeus (Luke 19:1-10). Even though a Jew, Zacchaeus collected taxes in Palestine for the Romans. The Romans assessed each province a certain amount of tax, and the tax collector's job was to raise it. If he did not raise the full amount, the rest came out of his pocket. If he raised more than the assessment, he pocketed the excess. Tax collectors set the rates high and never fell short on collections. Consequently, they lived the high life, in stark contrast to the people in Palestine.

Zacchaeus was a chief tax collector and very rich. News of Jesus of Nazareth, the teacher and healer who appeared to have a direct line to God, was spreading throughout Palestine. When Zacchaeus heard Jesus would be coming through Jericho, the taxman determined to catch a glimpse of the healer. Being short in stature, Zacchaeus climbed a sycamore tree to get a better view. When Jesus passed by, he noticed Zacchaeus in the tree and invited himself to dinner. Zacchaeus was flabbergasted. No one, other than other tax collectors, wanted anything to do with him. The people hated him for gouging them out of their hard-earned money, yet Jesus wanted to spend time with him.

Zacchaeus scrambled down the tree and escorted Jesus home. The encounter turned Zacchaeus's life upside down. We do not know what exactly transpired, but we do know that by the end of the meal Zacchaeus was moved to call Jesus "Lord," and to make amends for his greedy and gouging behavior.

And what amends he made! He gave half of his possessions to the poor. Every person he had defrauded received a four-fold repayment. After coming spiritually alive in Christ, Zacchaeus reflected on his behavior, noted the way he had hurt others, and set out to repair the damage he had done. In other words, he took Steps Eight and Nine!

The other pertinent Scripture passage comes from the Sermon on the Mount:

> So when you are offering your gift at the altar, if you remember that your brother or sister has something against you, leave your gift there before the altar and go; first be reconciled to your brother or sister, and then come and offer your gift. (Matthew 5:23-24)

Jesus asked his listeners to imagine coming to church with a gift for God. In those days it might have been a calf, a dove, or an offering of incense or grain; today it would probably be a monetary gift. But Jesus stated a condition: He did not want the gift if, right in the middle of the offering, we remembered we had injured or harmed someone and had not done what we could to make things right. Imagine what would happen if something similar happened in churches today. Imagine worship leaders making us sign a pledge before the offering each Sunday. The pledge form would read, "Have you done everything in your power to make amends to people you have hurt? Do you make a pledge that your relational slate is clean?" If we could not sign the form, we would be escorted out of the building and told not to come back until we had done all we could to foster reconciliation. Imagine how different churches would be, imagine how different we would be, and imagine how different the world would be if each of us would follow Jesus's mandate to identify those we have injured and make amends—to take Steps Eight and Nine. Who are the people we have harmed? To whom do we need to make amends? We need to look in three major areas: harming others, harming ourselves, and harming God.

Harming Others

The most obvious recipients of our injurious behavior are other people. We may have injured these folk *materially*. We may have borrowed money and not paid it back. We may have sold someone an inferior product we were glad to get off our hands. We may have borrowed a book and still have it on our bookshelf. We may have charged someone full price for something and provided only half the service. We may have charged the company for our personal calls or taken supplies without reimbursing the company. We may have hit someone's car in the parking lot and not left a note. We may have allowed others to pay, and we seldom, if ever, pick up the check. Or just the opposite: We may always pick up the check, making others feel inadequate. We're talking about any behavior that negatively affects other folk in a tangible way.

We may have injured people *morally*. For example, we may have asked someone for an answer on a test, placing that person in a moral bind. We may have asked our spouse to lie for us by calling the office and telling them we were sick when, in fact, we were not. We may have taken credit for a colleague's idea. We may have spread lies about a friend or co-worker behind his or her back. We may have been unethical in our business dealings. We may have broken a promise to someone who was counting on us.

We also may have injured people *emotionally*. We may have held back from sharing ourselves fully with family members, making them feel less than worthy. We may have verbally abused people in private or public, wounding their spirit. We may have led people on, causing them to think we loved them when we really did not, and broken their heart. We may have given our parents a number of sleepless nights worrying about our rebelliousness. We may have disappointed our children by missing their concerts, plays, recitals, or games.

Whatever the injury—material, moral, physical, or emotional—Steps Eight and Nine call us to perform relational "housecleaning." These Steps ask us to identify the ways in which we have injured other people and see what we can do to heal the hurt we have caused.

Harming Ourselves

It may sound strange, but many of us have hurt ourselves more than we have anyone else. We may mercilessly put ourselves down. We may punish ourselves abusively when we fall short of some expectation or goal. If only we could have been more loving, more understanding, more sensitive, better prepared, smarter, stronger, or more outgoing. We may not have been very loving or forgiving to the person who lives inside our skin.

During a three-month leave from pastoral ministry, I saw a therapist weekly. I did not know if I would return to parish ministry. The responsibilities seemed overwhelming. I wanted out. I didn't know what I would do if I left pastoring; I just knew I was dying inside trying to keep all the balls in the air. The therapist told me quite emphatically that I had a major problem. (Great! That's exactly what you want your therapist to tell you!) He said I had an internal "bully." Inside of myself was someone who would beat me up every time I did not perform perfectly. He unveiled a recording I played in my mind that came from my mother. Every time I did something wrong, my mother would say, "If only you had used common sense, this would not have happened." Those words resulted in a personal expectation that I be "omniscient," that I know everything: every need, every expectation, and every answer. When I did not know, when I disappointed someone, the recording went off in my head: "If only you had seen this coming. Anyone with common sense would have planned for this. What's wrong with you?"

My therapist introduced me to someone else inside of me. While giving me tools to keep the bully at bay, he reminded me that someone precious—a nice, kind, conscientious, and responsible me—also lives inside. My therapist asked me to start seeing myself through the eyes of Christ instead of the eyes of the internal bully.

Taking Steps Eight and Nine may require us to make amends to ourselves. We may need to stop blaming ourselves for unreasonable expectations and events we can't control. We may need to apologize to ourselves for treating ourselves so harshly.

Harming God

We also may need to make amends to God. When asked to identify the greatest commandment, Jesus replied, "You shall love the Lord your God with all your heart, and with all your soul, and with all your mind. This is the greatest and the first commandment" (Matthew 22:37-38). God wants our love, and we hurt God when we fail to love without reservation.

Amazingly, God has feelings too. Scripture records offense after offense against God that reveal God's aching heart:

When Israel was a child, I loved him,
and out of Egypt I called my son.
The more I called them, the more they went from me;
they kept sacrificing to the Baals, and offering incensed to idols.

Yet it was I who taught Ephraim to walk, I took them up in my arms;
but they did not know that I healed them.

I led them with cords of human kindness, with bands of love.

I was to them like those who lift infants to their cheeks.

I bent down to them and fed them.

How can I give you up, Ephraim? How can I hand you over, O Israel?

How can I make you like Admah? How can I treat you like Zeboiim?

My heart recoils within me; my compassion grows warm and tender.

I will not execute my fierce anger; I will not again destroy Ephraim;

for I am God and no mortal, the Holy One in your midst,

and I will not come in wrath. (Hosea 11:1-4, 8-9)

We could easily substitute our name for Ephraim and Israel. We, too, have hurt God, and God's heart is breaking. We need to come before God with our humble apology.

A Heavy Sack to Carry

A psychology professor told each of her students to bring a clear plastic bag and a sack of potatoes to class. She instructed her students to call to mind every person they had harmed. For every person they had disappointed or hurt, they were to write his or her name on a potato and put the potato in the plastic bag.

They were told to carry this bag with them everywhere, putting it beside their bed at night, on the car seat when driving, on their lap when riding, next to their desk during classes, even taking it with them on dates. As you can imagine, the bag was pretty heavy. Lugging it around, paying attention to it all the time, and remembering not to leave it in embarrassing places became a hassle. Over time, the potatoes became moldy, smelly, and began to sprout "eyes."

With our sack of smelly potatoes, we move on to Step Nine.

Obstacles in the Way

One would think that with a bunch of smelly relationships stinking up our lives, we would be raring to take Step Nine. We would be ready to make amends and stop the stench. Unfortunately, the opposite is often true. We find making amends as repulsive as the smelly potatoes. We dread the thought of having to do it. Making amends runs contrary to almost every instinct we possess.

One defining moment in the spiritual journey of the best-selling author John Grisham came several years after graduating from Mississippi State University, when one of his classmates in law school revealed that he was terminally ill. John asked him, "What do you do when you realize you are about to die?"

The friend replied, "It's real simple. You get things right with God, and you spend as much time with those you love as you can. Then you settle up with everybody else."

Why do we often wait so long to "settle up"? Why don't we settle up now so we can live more abundantly and joyfully in the present? Why do we find making amends so distasteful? Three obstacles come to mind.

Ego

The first obstacle to making amends is our ego. Ashleigh Brilliant, who scribbled his offbeat humor on hippie postcards in the seventies, once penned: "All I ask of life is a constant and exaggerated sense of my own importance." Making amends threatens our self-importance. Making amends runs the risk of dropping us down a notch or two in others' eyes, and our ego fights back. Our ego says, "I don't want to blow my image of being a wonderful person." Or it says, "I am just plain scared of looking someone in the eye, saying I've wronged them, and apologizing. I don't know if I could handle my embarrassment or that person's anger." Or the ego says, "Come on, I haven't really harmed anyone. Who have I hurt? I'm a pretty decent person." Or the ego says, "Okay, I may have harmed someone, but that's nothing compared to what that other guy did to me. He started it. He's guiltier than I am. Let *him* apologize!" Because of our ego, we are tempted to take a pass on Step Nine.

Others

Second, there is the problem with others. Simply put, our efforts at reconciliation may be rebuffed. We may experience what a mother experienced with her daughter. The mother became very angry, and in the heat of the moment said some things to her daughter that she later regretted. After calming down, she went upstairs to her daughter's room, knocked on the door, and said, "Honey, can I come in? I want to apologize for what I said."

The daughter opened the door a crack and said, "No, you can't come in. I am not through being mad at you yet."

Sometimes it's going to be like that. Sometimes, no matter what we do, we may not be able to make things right. If we think or feel that may occur, we need to remember the counsel of the Apostle Paul: "If it is possible, so far as it depends on you, live peaceably with all" (Romans 12:18). According to Paul, we can only clean up our side of the street. What people decide to do on their side of the street is another matter. Some people will refuse to forgive us. While that might be difficult to accept, we can live more peacefully knowing we did everything in our power to bring healing to the relationship.

In two full pages of advertisement, the Japanese government declared its desire to right wrongs committed in World War II. The Asian Women's Fund, led by former Japanese Prime Minister Tomiichi Murayama, placed the ads to announce the offer of atonement payments to "comfort women" who were forced to provide sexual services to members of Japan's wartime military. In an effort to make atonement, the organization sent them donations, messages, and a letter of apology from the Prime Minister.

Murayama wrote, "We hope these projects have helped to remove at least some portion of the permanent scars these women bear. I consider it essential that we Japanese maintain a firm conviction that we must never violate the dignity of women again, as we did in our treatment of 'comfort women.'"

Some responded positively to the offer of atonement payments. Others did not. What was important was that, in a nation of "face-saving," the government acted out of character. They took a risk, knowing they could never put things right, and that some would refuse their apology altogether. But they did what they could to clean up their side of the street.

Circumstances

The third obstacle to taking the Ninth Step has to do with circumstances. We may not be able to make amends to an injured party. Some may have moved away, and we cannot locate them. Some may be too ill to see anyone. Some people may have died.

That was the case with my father. My parents divorced when I was six years old, and my mother received custody of my sister and me. My father had weekend visitation privileges. At the age of eleven, I refused to visit my father. Why? Because I wanted him to put a swimming pool in his backyard, and he decided against it. I was furious. We lived in Southern California. It was the thing to do—at least in the eyes of an eleven-year-old boy who loved the water. I wanted a swimming pool, and I thought he could afford one, but he refused. So for six months I refused to visit him on weekends. I even refused to speak to him on the phone when he called.

Then I saw a baseball glove I just *had* to have. It cost forty-five dollars, which was a lot of money in 1959. I asked my mother for a loan, and she wisely said, "Ask your dad." So I called him and asked for a loan. He didn't harangue me for calling only when I wanted something. He didn't scold me for not speaking to him for six months. He simply asked, "How much do you need?" He bought me the glove. I started visiting him again, but we never spoke about the swimming pool, and I never apologized for my immature behavior.

After my father died, I stood by his open casket, realizing I had lost the chance to apologize to him. I tried. I looked into the casket and said, "Dad, I'm sorry for what I did. I was only eleven, but that is not an excuse." He could not reply. He was gone. I had missed my chance. The moral? We need to get after making amends because the circumstances may make it impossible later. Of course, if we have missed our chance, all hope is not lost. Some have found it helpful to write a letter to a deceased person and read it aloud, or to visit their grave to say how sorry they were for their behavior. While not quite as satisfactory as an eye-to-eye encounter, a belated apology has brought much needed closure for many people.

Incentives Along the Way

While the obstacles (ego, others, circumstances) may be formidable, the benefits of doing Step Nine make overcoming the obstacles worth the effort, humiliation, and pain. The biggest reward? We get that sack of potatoes off our back.

Early in his career Jackie Gleason performed at a seaside resort in New Jersey, and he rented a room in a boarding house for the season. The owner of the boarding house sat behind a desk at the front of the stairs. She saw to it that no one left without paying.

When the engagement ended, Gleason was told his paycheck would be mailed to him the following week. He needed, however, to pay for his room, and he had no money. How was he going to get past the old woman without paying?

Gleason came up with an idea. He called a couple of friends in New York City and asked for their help. When they arrived, he lowered his suitcases out the back window into their car. He then squeezed into his bathing suit and went down the front staircase. The woman nodded. Gleason gave her a big smile, and said, "Nice day for a dip in the ocean." Then he walked out, turned the corner, climbed into the waiting car, and sped toward New York City with his friends.

Two weeks later, he was working at a club and making good money. He thought of the woman who ran the boarding house and began to feel guilty. His conscience told him he needed to make restitution. The next day he drove to the Jersey shore and strode into the boarding house with the money in hand. Sure enough, the owner of the boarding house was behind the desk. He gave her the money, and she unexpectedly burst into tears. "We thought you had drowned," she said!

Gleason explained himself, made things right, and afterward said that he felt like a million bucks.

We will not only feel better emotionally when we make amends, but we will also feel better spiritually. God cares deeply about relationships. When Jesus summarized the core of spirituality, he did so relationally: "Love God with all your heart, all your soul, and all your mind, *and love your neighbor as yourself.*" We might call the Kingdom of God the "Kingdom of Right Relationships"—right and healthy relationships with God, with self, and with others. What could please God more, then, than for us to care deeply about our relationships? If God lives in us, we will be driven to seek recon-ciliation. As God took the initiative with us, we will take the initiative with others. We will seek people out. We will do what we can to make things right. Some may not accept our offer, just as some have not accepted God's offer in Jesus Christ, but we will build and repair bridges wherever possible. And by making amends, by working on broken bridges, we will be doing what is at the center of God's heart. We will feel better spiritually because we have aligned ourselves with God's purpose in the world.

We may even feel better relationally. The movie *Beaches* tells the story of two women whose lifelong friendship bridged their opposite backgrounds and lifestyles. CC Bloom (Bette Midler), raised by a sin-gle, blue-collar mother, followed her childhood dream and became an actress and recording artist. Hillary Whitney (Barbara Hershey), raised in an affluent family, attended law school, married a successful lawyer, and enjoyed the privilege of wealth. The two remained friends until a breach of trust drove a wedge between them.

After Hillary's husband left her for another woman, Hillary heard that CC was a headliner at a nightclub in San Francisco, and Hillary found the courage to go and attempt to make amends. CC met Hillary with great hostility, blasting her for abandoning the friendship. Hillary countered by saying she was jealous of CC and had always felt inferior to her. After much verbal jousting, CC finally blurted out, "It was all my fault!" Realizing that the barrier had been broken between them, Hillary tearfully responded by saying, "It was all *our* fault."

While some of our relationships will not be healed by taking Step Nine, some will. We will rekindle friendships. We will laugh and cry again with people we have missed. The benefit of that far outweighs the cost of not taking this Step.

The Process

Our negative actions and behaviors can be corrected, and for our emo-tional, spiritual, and relational well-being, they need to be. When we are ready to take the "make up" Steps, here's what we need to do.

First, we ask God's help in identifying and remembering the people we have hurt. We will not be able to remember all of them on our own. We make a list of those people as God brings them to mind.

Second, we ask God for the willingness, sensitivity, and courage to make the amends. We think through what we want to say and do. We work on keeping the apology simple and direct, and we avoid blaming other people.

Third, we heed the warning in Step Nine: "except when to do so would injure them or others." We consider the question, "Am I making amends at the cost of another person's reputation, well-being, or privacy?" For example, if a woman had an affair with her best friend's husband, she would first need to get permission from the husband prior to making amends to her best friend.

Fourth, we go to people we have hurt, ask for forgiveness, and ask permission to make amends. We do not go with any expectations of how the people might respond to us. It may go well. It may not. Others may want to hold onto their anger or hatred toward us. We can only clean up our side of the street.

Fifth, we make amends. We do something to repair the damage. If we stole money, we pay it back. If we borrowed a tool, we return it. If we dropped the ball on an assignment, we ask for another assignment to complete the job. We do not stop short. We do not hold back as the shoplifter did who wrote to a department store and said, "I've just become a Christian, and I can't sleep at night because I feel guilty. So here's the $100 that I owe you." He signed his name, and then in a little postscript at the bottom he added, "If I still can't sleep, I'll send you the rest."

Few things are more desirable than a clear conscience. The "make up" Steps help us clear our conscience so we will not be weighed down by the memories of those we have harmed. These Steps enable us to heal the past so God might transform the future. They offer us the serenity and peace we seek.

Summary Points to Ponder

⊚ *Steps Eight and Nine are "reconciliation" Steps or "restitution" Steps. They ask us to make a list of people we have injured, attempt to heal the relationship, and make amends wherever possible.*

◉ *The most obvious recipients of our injurious behavior are other people. We may have injured others materially, morally, physically, or emotionally.*

◉ *It may sound strange, but many of us have hurt ourselves more than we have anyone else.*

◉ *We also may need to make amends to God. Amazingly, God has feelings, too.*

◉ *Why do we often wait so long to "settle up"? Why don't we settle up now so we can live more abundantly and joyfully in the present?*

◉ *While the obstacles may be formidable, the benefits of doing Step Nine make overcoming them worth the effort, humiliation, and pain.*

◉ *The "make up" Steps enable us to heal the past so that God might transform the future. They offer us the serenity and peace we seek.*

Personal Exercises

1. Read and meditate upon the following Scriptures:
   a. Matthew 5:23-26
   b. Luke 19:1-10
   c. Romans 12:18
   d. Psalm 51:14-17

2. Read over the Hosea passage (11:1-4, 8-9) three or four times, substituting your name for Israel and Ephraim. Monitor your feelings. How do you feel about God's love for you after doing this?

3. Begin to make a list of the people you have harmed. Start by dividing your life into five, ten, or fifteen year periods. Next to each name, write what harm you did them, as well as a possible means of making amends. Ask God's help in compiling the list and continue to add people as God brings them to your awareness.

4. How do circumstances affect your ability to make amends? What might you do to clear your conscience with these people?

Group Sharing and Discussion

1. Share a time when someone asked for your forgiveness. What were the circumstances? How did the request affect you emotionally? How did you feel about them afterward?

2. What grabbed your attention in this chapter?

3. From whom would you like to ask forgiveness or make amends, but circumstances keep you from being able to do so?

4. To whom do you need to extend forgiveness?

Section Four

The Keep It Up Steps

A doctor takes a patient's blood pressure; listens to his lungs; looks into his mouth, ears, and nose; reads his medical history chart; likes what he sees, and says, "You look great. Just keep doing what you are doing. I'll see you next year."

A teacher hands out book reports. Little Sarah receives a red letter "A" as well as a written comment at the top of the page: "Good work, Sarah. Keep it up."

A football team gets off to a 5-0 start. The sports commentator says, "They will go to the Super Bowl if they can just keep this up."

A woman goes to a weight loss clinic. The counselor notices her progress and says encouragingly, "Keep it up and you will lose those ten pounds before you know it."

A golfer computes his score after nine holes. He says to himself, "If I can keep this up for the back nine, I will break 90."

We move to the "Keep It Up" section of the Twelve Steps. Spiritual, emotional, relational, mental, and physical wholeness come from *continually* "giving up," "cleaning up," and "making up." We do not "give up," once and for all. Neither do we "clean up" nor "make up" just once. Because we continue to grab control, sin, and harm others, we need to continue "working the program," keeping up the gains we have made and not sliding back into old patterns and behaviors. The final three Steps enable us to stay grounded and growing in Christ.

Step 10: We continued to take personal inventory and when we were wrong promptly admitted it.

Step 11: We sought through prayer and meditation to improve our conscious contact with God *as we understood [God]*, praying only for knowledge of [God's] will for us and the power to carry that out.

Step 12: Having had a spiritual awakening as the result of these steps, we tried to carry this message to [others], and to practice these principles in all of our affairs.

Chapter 8

Ongoing Reflection and Repentance

Step 10: We continued to take personal inventory and when we were wrong promptly admitted it.

Andras Andreyevich Tamas served in the Hungarian Army under Nazi command during World War II. In 1944 the Second Hungarian Army (about 150,000 Hungarians) engaged the Soviet Red Army in the Don River region of the Soviet Union. An estimated ninety-thousand Hungarian soldiers died in battle. Tens of thousands perished in freezing temperatures trying to make it back to Hungary on foot. Tamas, at the age of nineteen, became a prisoner of war, and the Soviets sent him to Siberia.

In 1947 the Soviets released their prisoners of war, but not Tamas. Emaciated, disoriented, and combative, the Russians sent him to a state psychiatric hospital . . . and left him there for fifty-three years! Assuming he was German, hospital officials mistook his Hungarian language for the gibberish of a lunatic. Communication proved impossible. He did not understand Russian, and they did not know Hungarian. Decades passed. Finally, in 1999 a Slovak-born official working in a nearby children's penal colony recognized the words Tamas spoke as Hungarian.

Shortly thereafter psychiatrists at the hospital began to realize what had happened. Unfortunately, after decades of isolation in a state-run psychiatric hospital, Tamas had forgotten who he was. A Hungarian psychiatrist from Budapest came to the rescue. Exhibiting great patience over a three-day period, Dr. Andras Veer helped Tamas recover his memories. On August 11, 2000, Tamas returned home to Budapest as a war hero, "the last prisoner of World War II."

Not only had Tamas forgotten who he was, but he also hadn't seen his own face in five decades. So, according to one news account, upon returning to Budapest the old man spent hours studying his face in the mirror, staring into his deep-set eyes, inspecting the gray stubble on his chin and the furrows of his brow. It was his face, but after fifty-three years, it was a startling revelation. He hardly recognized himself.

After working through the first nine Steps, we may not recognize ourselves either. The changes God has made, and is making in us, are profound. A transformation has been taking place. We still sin, we still have those character defects, but we are getting better. We do not feel as out of control. Our lives seem more manageable. We feel much saner. Our relationships have improved. Letting go and letting God has been one of the best decisions of our lives, and friends and family have begun to notice the change in us as well. We hear things such as, "You seem so much more at peace," or "I don't know what's been going on, but I like the changes," or "You are so much easier to be around these days. What's happened to you?"

What has happened is that we have embarked on a courageous process of spiritual renewal. We have turned control of our lives over to God. With God's help we have examined ourselves inside and out. We have noted our strengths and our defects. We have thanked God for the good within us and asked God to remove the flaws that adversely affect us and others. Some of those flaws are not as pronounced as they once were. We've even gone so far as to apologize to others for the times we've hurt them and asked how we might make amends for the damage we've inflicted. We may not be hitting on all cylinders, but we are close. We feel as good about ourselves as we've ever felt. We feel good about our relationship with ourselves, with God, and with others.

Our New House

Good . . . Great . . . Terrific . . . Super . . . and keep it up! Imagine buying a house, a fixer-upper. You know the house is in disrepair, but you also see the potential. Yes, there are cracks in the foundation. Yes, the basement is bowing, the wood is rotting, and the porch is leaning, but you can see what the house can become. So you repair the foundation. You buttress the basement; you replace the wood and strengthen the porch. You paint, tile, carpet, and wallpaper, and the house looks wonderful. People walk into the house, and they feel "the magic." "What a beautiful home!"

We have done something similar in the first nine Steps: We have repaired our "house." In Steps One through Three, we did our foundation work. We decided to build our house on God's adequacy not our inadequacy. We said to God, "I admit I am powerless over sin, but God, you have the power, so I'm going to turn my life over to you." With that strong foundation in place, we moved to the structure of our house. In Steps Four through Nine, we fixed up the house. We did a moral inventory. We looked at where the walls were strong and where they were weak. We asked God's help in changing. Then we cleaned everything, saying, "If there is anyone I've offended, I will make amends."

Now our house looks radically different. It sparkles. It shines. It's ready for us to enjoy. So, why not stop here? Why do we need additional Steps? We need them because after doing the first nine Steps, it's easy to say, "I'm done. This was great. Thank you very much. I am a different person. There is no more to do." So we move into the house, but we do not keep it up. The house falls into disrepair once again. The Apostle Paul warned us about this: "So, if you think you are standing, watch out that you do not fall" (1 Corinthians 10:12). In other words, if we think we are all done, watch out. Sure, our house is better than it has ever been, but if we do not perform regular cleaning and maintenance, our house is going to end up like it was when we started. The final three Steps teach us how to live in the house. They teach us about home maintenance.

Step Ten

Step Ten reads: *We continued to take a personal inventory and when we were wrong, promptly admitted it.*

The Apostle Paul wrote, "Test everything; hold fast to what is good; abstain from every form of evil" (1 Thessalonians 5:21–22). I wish he had not used the word "test." Few of us look forward to taking a test, whether it is a driver's test, a blood test, or calculus test. I have nightmares about tests. I've been out of college and seminary for years, but I sometimes dream I am back in college taking a test, and I am unprepared because I have not attended class the entire semester. It's an awful nightmare. When I awake, I breathe a great sigh of relief, and think, "Whew, it was only a dream! I'm no longer in school." It doesn't matter whether I'm prepared or unprepared; I do not look forward to a test. But that is what the Tenth Step asks us to do: to test our actions on a regular basis; to take a personal inventory on a regular basis, to pay attention to how we are living *on a regular basis.*

What the Apostle Paul said after "test everything," however, makes this process a little more attractive. He went on to say, "Hold on to what is good." In other words, focus on more than the negative. The personal inventory is not done only in red ink. It's a bizarre day when we have done *nothing* right. The regular inventory does look for character defects, sins, and failures—*and* for the good we accomplish. Think of it as engaging in ongoing personal reflection. We can do this in a number of ways.

Spot Check Inventory

One way to take a quick inventory is to make "spot checks" during the day. Some even set their digital watches to go off hourly to analyze their behavior, thoughts, and emotions. Here are a few suggestions that might work for you.

The HALT Approach

Some people pause several times a day to ask themselves, "Am I feeling Hungry, Angry, Lonely, or Tired?" These four markers alert us to warning signs of trouble. The way we take care of ourselves—or don't take care of ourselves—often shows up in physical and emotional ways. When we are hungry, angry, lonely, or tired, we are more likely to engage in inappropriate behavior than when we are satisfied, calm, connected, and rested. Monitoring these four areas of our lives can keep us focused and centered throughout the day.

The "Vital Signs" Approach

Some people take a quick inventory by checking five vital signs. Just as a doctor checks our pulse, blood pressure, and temperature, we can check five critical vital signs of wholeness: physical, emotional, mental, relational, and spiritual. First, we do a little *physical* inventory. We ask, "What's going on with my body? Is my stomach growling, churning, or tight? Does my head ache? Are my back, neck, or shoulders tight? Am I feeling tired or fatigued?" What's going on with our bodies often indicates a present problem or predicts a coming issue. For instance, my friends and family tell me that if I am biting my lower lip, that's a tip off that I am upset about something. If they see me biting, they give me a wide berth. So if I do a spot check physical inventory and realize I'm biting my lip, I know I'm uptight about something. That's a signal I need to go back to Step Three and turn whatever is bothering me over to God.

But our inventory doesn't stop with the physical; we go on to check our *emotional* state: "What am I feeling: mad, sad, glad, scared, excited, or tender? How come? What has triggered those feelings?" Then we do a *mental* inventory: "What's filling my mind? What am I noodling around and around in my head? Where is my mental energy focused? Am I being positive or negative? Am I saying good things to myself or am I beating myself up?" We follow that with a quick *relational* inventory: "How am I doing with my spouse, children, significant other, boss, co-workers, and friends? Is there anything strained right now between me and someone else? Is there anything that requires immediate attention?" Finally, we take a quick *spiritual* inventory: "How am I doing with God? Am I feeling close to God? Distant? Ashamed? Why? Do I trust God? Am I giving God control of my day?"

The Crisis Approach
When we find ourselves in a time of crisis, or discord, it is a good time to take a spot check inventory. We look away from the offending person or circumstance and focus on ourselves, checking to see if old character defects are surfacing at the moment. For example, a family member criticizes us, and we begin to get angry. We offer a rebuttal. We try to convince them that they have misjudged us. We find ourselves feeling hurt and angry at the same time. At this point, we step back and do a little inventory. We ask ourselves, "How do I usually act when I am criticized? How am I acting now? Do I want to respond as I usually do? Do I want to give in to this character defect or do I want to cooperate with God and act differently? How can I let go and let God in this situation?"

However we choose to do it, performing multiple, daily spot checks enables us to live in the moment by staying present mentally, physically, spiritually, emotionally, and relationally.

Daily Inventory

Some people choose to do an ongoing personal inventory at the end of each day or at the beginning of the next day. In a daily inventory, we review what has taken place in the past twenty-four hours and compile a balance sheet, summarizing the good and the bad.

Here's how I do it. Every morning I take out a journal and have a short time of reflection. At the top of my journal page, I list three things. I look over the past twenty-four hours and make a list of what I call "Grace-Filled Moments." I think back on the past day and list the good things, the surprises God gave me. On a typical day I might list: lunch with my daughter, a walk with Trudy, bumping into a friend at the grocery store, a new book, or a movie I enjoyed. Next, I list those times I fell short and moments I wish I could re-live differently. I call this my "Do Over" list. If I could have a "do-over," I would think, act, or react differently. Third, I list the good things I did over the previous twenty-four hours. I title this my "Atta Boy" list, and I include my good-guy acts or thoughts.

Another way of doing a daily inventory is to list our most common character defects (such as selfishness, impatience, rigidity, anger) and check to see if any of these defects have been operating in the past twenty-four hours. Others find that asking themselves a bunch of pointed questions is helpful: "When did I give or receive the most love today? When did I give or receive the least? When was I the happiest? When was I the saddest? What were the high point and the low point of the past twenty-four hours?"

One woman said of her daily inventory experience, "I do my Tenth Step every evening. It's become almost a ritual. I sit and close my eyes with the TV and everything off, and I go over the events of the day in my mind. I ask myself if there were things I could have done differently. Did I ruffle anyone's feathers or forget to say a simple thank you? I also review any situations where I got upset. How did I handle that? In any case, I want to make sure I'm leaving yesterday behind me. If I owe anyone a thank you or an apology, I jot it down and put the note on my mirror. That way I'll see it first thing in the morning and be sure to remember to set things right the very next day."

Whatever approach we choose, doing a daily inventory keeps us in touch with the movement of God. We see what God is doing, and still needs to do, in our lives.

Periodic Inventory

People approach housecleaning differently. Some, like me, are constant cleaners. They walk around with a duster in their hands. They constantly straighten up. As soon as they wake up in the morning, they make their bed. Others clean daily. They straighten up in the morning or before going to bed. Others prefer more periodic cleaning. They can handle a little more clutter and only clean once a week, or once a month, or do a major cleaning once or twice a year.

If we are constant cleaners, we will probably prefer the "spot check" inventory method. We want to stay on top of things and not let anything get by us. If we are daily cleaners, straightening up before we go to bed or before we leave for the office, we will probably gravitate toward doing a daily inventory. Straightening ourselves out day by day is more than enough for us. Then there are those who would rather clean only when things start to pile up. For those of us who prefer this method, a periodic inventory may be the ticket. We try to get away for an hour or two once a week, month, or quarter for our searching and fearless moral inventory. Too much naval gazing turns us off. We can see more progress over an extended period of time, so we prefer days, weeks, and/or months between each inventory.

Living in the Light

It does not matter how often we do our inventory: constantly, daily, weekly, monthly, quarterly, or semi-annually. It just matters that we do it, and that we do it regularly. We need to stay in touch with what is happening in our lives. Transformation occurs to the degree that we face the truth about ourselves, both negative and positive. In the past we might have hesitated to do this. Maybe we didn't do it at all. Or maybe we had trouble looking into our hearts and seeing the truth and are still living in the shadows of denial. God, however, offers us another option: "If we walk in the light as he is in the light, we have fellowship with one another, and the blood of Jesus his Son cleanses us from all sin" (1 John 1:7).

Jesus referred to himself as "The Light of the World." Ponder that image: The Light of the World. What does light do? It guides. It reveals. It comforts. Who wants to be without a flashlight during a power outage? Who wants to stumble around in the dark? We tread cautiously in the dark. We hear strange noises in the dark. Creatures come out of hiding in the dark. Things go "bump in the night." In the midst of darkness, however, comes hope. A light shines. A Guiding Light. A Revealing Light. A Comforting Light.

Twenty-seven-hundred years ago, King Ezechia had a huge problem: The city's water supply was outside the city's walls. This made Jerusalem vulnerable to enemy attacks, since Jerusalem's enemies could place the city in crisis by cutting off its water supply without ever entering the city. King Ezechia's solution was to build a tunnel. The Israelites tunneled seventeen-hundred feet through a solid rock mountain to bring water within the city walls. Construction of the tunnel started at both ends in the hope of meeting in the middle. The tunnel had a number of zigs and zags in it, but they accomplished the task. Today tourists can walk through King Ezechia's tunnel (although I would not recommend it to anyone who suffers from claustrophobia). One man described what it was like for him:

> I put on a bathing suit, entered the tunnel and began to wade through water that's waist-high, sometimes chest-high, and even higher. I carried a candle to light the way, as is the custom, and it became very scary at times because at some points along the way, the rock ceiling above and the water below leaves just enough room for your head in between. And there I was about half-way through, with over 800 feet to daylight in either direction—and my candle went out. The group I was with went on, turned a few corners and they were gone, and I was alone, in the eerie darkness. It just moved in to overwhelm me. I thought it was going to consume me. Rationally, there was no reason for the panicky fear that I felt because I knew that sooner or later the group would miss me and someone would come back for me. I reached out for the side of the tunnel and tried to feel my way along for a while as the darkness just poured over me like huge waves. And then, coming back, slowly picking his way was the guide carrying his candle. It was just a tiny little light, but how brightly it was shining for me! And when we finally stumbled out into the Pool of Siloam . . . I understood, as I never understood before, what Christ was talking about when he said, "I am the Light of the world. He who follows me will never walk in darkness but will have the Light of life."[25]

Our personal tunnels have been just as dark. Our flaws and shortcomings have threatened to drown us. But we never walk into that tunnel alone. The Light, Jesus Christ, goes with us. That's why it's so important to keep turning our lives and wills over to the Light. We could become overwhelmed in the tunnel. We could feel claustrophobic, closed in by the darkness within us. But if we walk in the Light, the Light will protect us. The Light will guide us. The Light will comfort us and heal us. We will have the courage to face ourselves—on a regular basis—because we know that whatever we discover about ourselves in the tunnel, whatever hollows of character defects or flaws we find, Christ gives us the power to overcome them. The promise cannot be clearer: If we walk in the light as he is in the light . . . he cleanses us from our sin. We cannot afford to walk in the darkness of denial if we want to maintain a healthy lifestyle. We cannot expect to grow spiritually if we keep things hidden.

Admitting It Promptly

The Tenth Step not only stresses taking a regular personal inventory, but also emphasizes *"when wrong promptly admit it."* Now, that's a challenge. We might not mind admitting mistakes we made ten or twenty years ago. We might have little difficulty admitting "Yep, back in 1992, I really messed up. I shouldn't have dropped out of college" or "I really blew it with my first wife. I hope I never repeat those mistakes with anyone else." Most of us do not have a problem admitting mistakes from the distant past. It's the ones we committed an hour ago that are a problem.

On a Father's Day I asked my wife, "Trudy, what do you think I inherited from my father?"

She asked, "What do you mean?"

I clarified, "I mean character traits and defects. In what way am I like my father?"

She answered, "Well, you look a lot like him physically, especially your facial features. You take good care of your possessions like your dad. You show affection by teasing like your father . . . and you have trouble forgiving people like your father."

Trudy was right. I picked up a defective gene from the Meyer side of the family. I loved my dad. I thought, and still think, he was a wonderful man, but he had a big problem with forgiveness. In fact, he was a world-champion grudge carrier. He might even be in the *Guinness Book of World Records* right alongside "The Most Drumbeats in a Minute" (1,080 by UK's Oliver Butterworth on June 13, 2002), the "Largest

Spider" (male goliath bird-eating spider, 11 inches), and the "Most Tornadoes in Twenty-Four Hours" (148 from Texas to Iowa to Nebraska on April 3-4, 1974).

When he was in his late teens, my father got into a squabble with his father over the family farm, and he joined the Marine Corps to get away. They never spoke another word to each other. As a result, I never met my paternal grandfather or grandmother. In his forties my father stopped speaking to one of his sisters—they had argued over a game of pinochle. When my father died some twenty years later, she refused to come to the funeral. She was just as stubborn and unforgiving as my father.

When he was in his late fifties, and on his third marriage, my father even stopped speaking to me for a while. He was angry because I wanted to maintain a relationship with his second wife, a woman with whom I had spent many a weekend after my parents divorced. She was a second mother to me, and I did not want to lose that relationship. He told me to choose her or him; I could not have both. I told him I would not choose between them. He stopped speaking to me for six months, until I finally flew to his home in Reno, Nevada, and told him he was being ridiculous. He never did apologize for cutting me out of his life, but at least he started speaking to me again, even though I continued my relationship with my stepmother.

My wife has to put up with this defective gene of mine: Like my father, I think it's the other person who is at fault, not me. Trudy and I seldom argue, but when we do, I am seldom the person to make it right. Ninety percent of the time, Trudy takes the initiative in patching things up. I can go for days without mending fences. It's a defective, stubborn, unforgiving gene that I carry. Promptly admitting I am wrong does not come naturally to me.

The practice of promptly admitting our wrongdoings is a terrific way to put out conflict fires before they get big. One man said, "I know I'm not perfect. Having Step Ten as part of my daily program of recovery keeps me from letting things build up. I've learned it's easier in the long run to make quick, simple amends as soon as they are due. At work, people now say I'm a caring, thoughtful, polite kind of a guy. That feels a whole lot better than what they used to call me."

It also helps to admit things promptly because we may have misjudged the impact of our actions on others. We may be carrying a bit of guilt for the way we treated someone, only to discover there was no reason to feel guilty. We may have thought we were insensitive or overbearing or curt with someone, when we actually were not. Acting promptly not only puts out fires before they get big, but it also quickly clears up any misconceptions we may have about our behavior. Most of us can think of times when we said to someone, "I'm sorry for the way I acted yesterday. I was terse, and I shouldn't have taken out the stress of my day on you," to which the person responded, "I didn't experience that at all. Don't think another minute about it." We had misread the situation. We were harder on ourselves than we needed to be.

I like the way one person summarized Step Ten: "Becoming self-aware is what Step Ten is to me. I never used to see the good things I did or give myself any credit. In just the same way, I never used to understand why I'd tick people off. Sometimes I did, but on the small things I usually didn't even notice. This new lifestyle takes constant practice. It's not all that natural feeling to me yet, but it's getting easier all the time."

May it become easier for all of us.

Summary Points to Ponder

◉ *We have embarked on a courageous process of spiritual renewal. We have worked through the first nine Steps. Now we need to keep up the gains we have made.*

◉ *In the first nine Steps we have repaired our "house." The final three Steps teach us how to live in the house. They teach us about home maintenance.*

◉ *The regular inventory not only checks for character defects, sins, and failures, but also looks for the good we accomplish.*

◉ *It does not matter how often we do our inventory: constantly, daily, weekly, monthly, quarterly, or semi-annually. It just matters that we do it, and that we do it regularly.*

*   *We cannot afford to walk in the darkness of denial if we want to maintain a healthy lifestyle. We cannot expect to grow spiritually if we keep things hidden. If we walk in the Light, the Light will protect us. The Light will guide us. The Light will comfort us and heal us.*

*   *Most of us do not have a problem admitting mistakes from the distant past. It's the ones we committed an hour ago that are a problem.*

*   *When we get into the practice of promptly admitting our wrong-doings, we put out conflict fires before they get big and quickly clear up any misconceptions we may have about our behaviors.*

Personal Exercises

1. Meditate upon the following Scriptures:
   a. 1 John 1:3-7
   b. 1 Corinthians 10:12
   c. 1 Corinthians 11:28
   d. 1 Thessalonians 5:21-22 *"Hold on to what is good."*
   e. Philippians 3:12-14
   Forgetting the past and looking forward to what lies ahead

2. Which method of ongoing regular personal inventory will you likely do?
   a. Spot Check.
   b. Daily.
   c. Periodic.
   d. Weekly.
   e. Monthly.
   f. Quarterly.
   h. Semi-annually.
   i. Combination of the above.

Group Sharing and Discussion

1. What do you remember about going to bed at night as a child? Night light? Monsters under the bed? Crawling into bed with Mom or Dad? A stuffed animal?

2. What recently received your prompt attention? How quickly did you act upon it? What does this tell you about your willingness to take care of things promptly?
   a. A business call.
   b. A crisis at home or office.
   c. A news report.
   d. A sporting event.
   e. A letter or bill in the mail.
   f. A doctor's report.
   g. Other.

3. What spoke to you from this chapter?

4. Take five minutes of silence to do a quick personal inventory. Reflect on the day's activities. Make a list of your accomplishments and wrongdoings. Share one accomplishment and one wrongdoing from your day with group members.

Chapter 9

Staying in Touch with God

Step 11: We sought through prayer and meditation to improve our conscious contact with God *as we understood [God],* **praying only for knowledge of [God's] will for us and the power to carry that out.**

A friend and former co-worker, Marshall Ziemann, shared this memory of his childhood: "My brother, Mark, and I would spend the night at our friend Tim's house. We never really had friends sleep over at our house. My folks liked things quiet, but for us Tim's folks were perfect. Noise did not bother them. Once asleep they were out for the night.

"So at Tim's house we would stay awake for hours past our normal bedtime. Sometimes we would watch television. Sometimes we would play bumper pool, which Tim always won. But by far the best activity we ever did at Tim's house was listening to a big, old radio in his basement, the kind of radio that had different bands and frequencies. We went back and forth through the dials, listening to see what was out there.

"I say 'seeing' because as I stared into the tubes of that old radio, in my mind I could see those people sitting in studios in far-off lands. We put a map on the wall with pins of every place of which we heard. We would all take turns spinning the dial, listening mostly to static, jotting down different frequencies, relentless in our efforts to try to make contact with someone.

"I say 'trying' to make contact with someone. Actually, we never were able to make contact with anyone. We never were broadcasting anything. Nobody ever knew we were listening in. We did not have a transmitter. We did not have a microphone. Our communication was never two-way. We just received whatever we happened to pick up. That was as good as it ever got: hit and miss, good nights and bad nights, an occasional flurry of brilliant reception with lots of hours of poor reception in between."[26]

We might say the same thing about our attempts to make contact with God: "Good nights and bad nights, an occasional flurry of brilliant reception with lots of hours of poor reception in between." A long-time church member confessed, "All my life I have prayed, but I have had very little actual contact with God." Many of us can echo that person's confession. We may have prayed consistently and regularly but have had very little actual contact with the Almighty. Prayer is a difficult discipline. We know it is something we should be doing, but we sometimes feel we must be doing something wrong because we seem to have trouble making contact with God.

Step Eleven

Step Eleven attempts to change that. Step Eleven encourages us to scan the airways of heaven and "dial in" to God. The Eleventh Step reads: *We sought through prayer and meditation to improve our conscious contact with God, praying only for knowledge of [God's] will for us and the power to carry that out.* This Step is very straightforward. It invites us to build an intimate, spiritual relationship with God. In many ways it resonates with the words of the Apostle John:

We declare to you what was from the beginning, what we have heard, what we have seen with our eyes, what we have looked at and touched with our hands, concerning the word of life—this life was revealed, and we have seen it and testify to it, and declare to you the eternal life that was with the Father and was revealed to us—we declare to you what we have seen and heard so that you also may have fellowship with us; and truly our fellowship is with the Father and with his Son Jesus Christ. We are writing these things so that our joy may be complete. (1 John 1:1-4)

John stressed two points. First, he stated that Jesus was the real deal. John had heard him. He had seen him. And most importantly, he had touched him. John stressed this to combat a heresy that was making inroads into the early church. Some people were saying that Jesus was a phantom or, in modern day lingo, Jesus was not much more than a hologram—a good hologram, perhaps the best hologram ever conceived, but a hologram nonetheless. So John wanted to make it clear that Jesus was no ghost, no phantom, no hologram. Jesus was the real deal.

Second, John stated that this "real deal" could be known and experienced by you and me. "We declare to you what we have seen and heard so that you also may have fellowship with us; and truly our fellowship is with the Father and with his Son Jesus Christ." The Greek word for fellowship is *koinonia* and refers to an "in-depth" type of relationship. In classical Greek it describes the most intimate of relationships. That's what John wanted for the people to whom he was writing—and for us: an intimate relationship with Jesus Christ.

It's Possible

The goal of Step Eleven is the same thing: to live in constant, conscious contact with God. Of course, the question is, "How do we do that? How do we make conscious contact with God? How do we develop an intimate relationship with Jesus Christ?"

First, we have to know it's possible.

I love the story about the wealthy resident of New York City who died and in her will left her entire estate to God. The will, of course, was contested by her would-be heirs and made its way to court. A lawsuit was started in which "God" was named as a party. A summons was issued, and the official process servers went through the motions of trying to serve it. The report they returned to court read as follows: "After a due and diligent search, made in accordance with established procedures, God cannot be found in New York City."

Do we live in a world where God cannot be found? Or do we live in a world where God acts, intrudes, moves, and speaks?

At one time, the number one requested song at funerals used to be "In the Garden." The lyrics go:

I come to the Garden alone while the dew is still on the roses,
And the voice I hear, falling on my ear, the Son of God discloses.
And he walks with me, and he talks with me, and he tells me
 I am his own;
And the joy we share as we tarry there, none other has ever
 known.[27]

I've often wondered why so many people chose this hymn, and I've come up with two educated guesses. Either they sang "In the Garden" at church as a child, and it brought back fond memories, or the hymn captured their experience with God. I venture to say that the second reason was probably the main reason. They chose the song because they experienced what Adam and Eve experienced in the original garden: God walking and talking with them in the cool of the evening or at the beginning of each day.

If we desire to make conscious contact with God, we need to know it's possible. We need to know that God "walks" with us and seeks an intimate, personal relationship with us.

Correct a Faulty Image of God

Second, to make conscious contact with God, we may need to correct our faulty image of God. A large part of how we approach God is how we see God. If we see God as disinterested in us, we won't want to bother God with our joys and concerns. If we see God as welcoming, we are more likely to approach God with confidence.

For many of us, our concept of God was formed by the early "power" people in our lives: parents, pastors, teachers, and coaches. What kind of pictures do we carry of those people, particularly our parents? Do we carry a picture of someone who is ready and eager to listen, or do we carry a picture of someone who would always say "just a minute" as they watched the news or read the newspaper? Do we carry a picture of someone who gave us the courage to reach beyond ourselves, or do we carry a picture of someone who did not see our potential? Do we carry a picture of someone who could be tender with us, or do we carry a picture of someone who laughed at us or teased us because of their insecurity? Do we carry a picture of someone who could make us the center of attention, or do we carry a picture of someone who did not notice us, or who wasn't around when we needed attention?

The Scriptures tell us we are created in the image of God, but many of us create God in the image of the early power people in our lives. What pictures of God do we carry in our wallet? We may have to replace some of our pictures with those from Scripture, borrowing pictures of God from the psalmist's experience:

> When they call to me, I will answer them;
> I will be with them in trouble,
> I will rescue them and honor them. (Psalm 91:15)

How close is this picture to the one we carry? Do we have a picture of a God who listens, answers, and acts on our behalf? Do we have a picture of God that looks like this: "The Spirit helps us in our weakness; for we do not know how to pray as we ought, but that very Spirit intercedes with sighs too deep for words" (Romans 8:26). Do we have a picture of God's Spirit praying for the deep desires and hurts of our souls? What about this picture of God: "The Lord is near. Do not worry about anything, but in everything by prayer and supplication with thanksgiving let your requests be made known to God" (Philippians 4:5-6). Do we have a picture of the Almighty who is so interested in every detail of our lives that we are to bring everything to God in prayer, not just the big things, but everything?

We need to replace our disinterested, distant, mean-spirited picture of God with one of God who deeply cares about us. We will be motivated to make conscious contact if we know we will be welcomed into God's presence.

Learn to Listen

Okay. We know it's possible to have an intimate relationship with God. Millions of people have had one; we can, too. We also know that God desires to spend time with us. We know that God is interested in every detail of our lives. So, how do we make contact?

The Eleventh Step says the way is through prayer and meditation. Is there a difference between the two? One person has suggested that prayer is conversing with God, while meditation is slowing down enough to hear God. Another says, "Prayer is asking and meditation is listening." Others say, "Prayer is science; meditation is art"; "prayer is rational; meditation is intuitive"; "prayer is logical; meditation is symbolic."[28]

While different, prayer and meditation share a similar requirement: the ability to listen. Prayer without listening is simply an exercise in control. Prayer without listening is simply telling God what we want or what we think God should know. When we pray without listening, we call all the shots. Prayer without listening is a one-way street. It's a monologue and not a dialogue.

Most of us, however, have not been taught how to listen to God. Most of us have been taught just the opposite. We have heard pastors, priests, rabbis, and church leaders say, "Let us pray," and then they began talking. For many of us, that has been our total experience of prayer. We may have been led to believe that meditation is for hippies or Eastern religion folk who wear robes, sit crossed-legged, and chant, "Oooommmm." In reality, meditation is simply an exercise in concentrated listening to God. For some, meditation involves getting up thirty minutes early, taking a cup of coffee to a quiet place, and just sitting and listening. For others, meditation involves turning off the radio on the way home or canceling a lunch and going for a walk alone. Meditation may involve putting the kids to bed, putting on a relaxing CD, and opening ourselves to whatever God wants to say to us.

For many of us, the fact that prayer involves listening, and meditation is for everyone, surprises us. We have not been exposed to the listening side of prayer. We do, however, see in Scripture that listening is an important element in making contact with God. In the book of Ecclesiastes, for example, we read, "To draw near to listen is better than the sacrifice offered by fools" (5:1). The psalmist adds, "Be still before the Lord, and wait patiently for him" (37:7).

Ever wonder how Jesus could spend the entire night in prayer? He could do it because he spent much of the night listening. Shortly after becoming a Christian, I decided to spend thirty minutes a day in prayer. What a disaster! The first day I went into my room, closed the door, checked the clock, and began to pray. I prayed for my family, my friends, myself, my upcoming year in college, the war in Vietnam, Governor Reagan, and President Nixon, the needy, the destitute, and the hungry. You name it, and I talked to God about it. When I finished, I thought, "Great! That must have taken at least thirty minutes." I looked at the clock and only seven minutes had elapsed. What was I going to do with the remaining twenty-three minutes? After all, I had made a commitment to God to pray thirty minutes a day. How do other people pray for so long?

They do it by talking to God *and* listening to God. They converse with God as they converse with others. How rude to talk the entire time and not listen to a friend or family member! The same applies to making contact with God. As in any healthy relationship, we need to listen as well as speak. Over the years I have found five practices to be especially helpful in learning how to listen.

The first is to divide time with God between speaking and listening. I started slowly, initially spending only three or five minutes listening, and then I gradually extended the time as I became more comfortable with silence. Setting aside time to listen revolutionized my conscious contact with God. I discovered the reason I had seldom heard God speak was because I hadn't been listening.

Second, at the beginning, give structure to the times of listening. I have found three listening exercises very helpful. One practice is to listen to God speak to me through God's creation. The Apostle Paul said of God, "Ever since the creation of the world his eternal power and divine nature, invisible though they are, have been understood and seen through the things he has made" (Romans 1:20). Every so often I choose something from the created order—a tree, plant, bird, leaf, cloud—and ponder it carefully and prayerfully. I ask God, "What do you want me to learn from this thing you have made?"

Another way is to listen to God through the Scriptures. I take a single event, such as the resurrection, or a parable, or a short passage, and allow it to take root inside of me. I close my eyes and, using all my senses, seek to have the Scripture come alive. I smell the sea. I hear the lap of the water along the shore. I see the crowd. I taste the salt in the air. I touch the hem of Jesus's garment. Then I ask God, "What do you want to say to me through this passage of Scripture?"

Another way of structuring the time involves closing my eyes and picturing myself in a favorite place, conversing with Jesus. Often that is the beach. I picture myself sitting on the shore, watching the waves break, and Jesus coming up and sitting alongside of me. We watch the surf together. We talk. I share what's bothering me and what excites me. These times have been marvelous as I've laughed, wept, and learned from the Risen Christ.

Third, give our wandering minds to Christ. One of the major roadblocks in being still and patiently waiting for God to speak is a wandering mind. We begin thinking about the upcoming events of our day, what we need to pick up at the grocery store on the way home, or something we said earlier in the day, and we become frustrated with ourselves. A wandering mind, however, is normal and can be used to our advantage. For example, when my mind wanders, I ask God, "Why is this happening? Why am I so preoccupied with what we are having for dinner?" This turns my attention back to God. Others find it helpful to have a notepad handy. When their mind starts to wander, they jot down the detour on the pad and get back to it after they have spent time listening to God.

Fourth, practice discerning the voice of Christ. Years ago we held a new member class in the church basement. The church nursery was located above our meeting room, and during the class we could hear any baby who cried. When that happened, some couple would turn to one another and grimace. They knew their baby's cry; they had heard it many times. I could not have told you whose baby was crying because I had not spent extensive time with that child, but the parents could. The same applies with our relationship with Christ. With practice, we will be able to discern the voice of Christ among the many thoughts that clamor for our attention.

Fifth, we should not expect God to speak every time we listen. On a good week I may feel in contact with God only a third of the times I set aside for prayer and meditation. Even during those silent times, however, I know I am doing something important. By setting aside time to listen, I am affirming my love of God. As a friend said, "We simply cannot love without listening." That's reason enough for most of us to practice listening prayer.

Seek God's Will Only for Our Lives

Through prayer and meditation, we not only seek an intimate relationship with God, but also God's guidance for our lives. The Eleventh Step directs us to pray for the knowledge of God's will "only" for ourselves. That word "only" is very important. When Jesus was with his disciples after the resurrection, he told Peter what was in store for him, and Peter asked, "What about John? What's going to happen to him?" Jesus said, and this is a rough paraphrase, "That's none of your business." In other words, "Focus on your side of the fence, Peter, not John's side of the fence. Keep your nose out of John's life. Keep your nose out of your spouse's life. Keep your nose out of your children's life. Pray for the knowledge of God's will only for *your* life."

That's a challenge because we think we know what others need. How presumptuous! We do not always know what we need! We have enough on our plates trying to fix our lives without trying to fix someone else's.

Have you ever heard of the sport "orienteering"? It's a game of following directions. Participants move about a mapped-out course with precision, speed, and unerring sense of direction. It requires the ability to take accurate compass readings and hike through the terrain. If you like treasure hunts and vigorous exercise, you would love this sport. For all the directionally-challenged among us, however, almost nothing sounds as tortuous as spending an entire day following directions such as, "Proceed one quarter mile at eight degrees southwest of the previous checkpoint." For some, orienteering has made an enjoyable sport out of the art of navigation; for the directionally-disabled, it's a surefire way to get frustrated, confused, and hopelessly lost.

Thankfully, even for folks with no sense of direction, there's a method for determining how to read and follow a moral compass. There's a guide for the growth of our souls: through prayer and meditation we find out what God wants us to do. Norman Vincent Peale wrote,

> By prayer, you may receive guidance in all the problems and enter-prises of life. And this will lead you to right decisions about everything in which you are concerned. It is an enormous blessing to realize that you can have the directive guidance of the vast intelligence of God. This should materially reduce the mistake and error quotient in your experience.[29]

Seek the Power to Carry It Out

The knowledge of God's will for our lives is one thing. The power to carry it out is another. It's through prayer and meditation that we receive this power.

While on the mission field, Herb Jackson was assigned a car. The car, however, would not start without a push. Pondering the situation, Jackson devised a plan. He would go to the school near his home and "borrow" some children to push the car to get it started. Then he would make his rounds for the day, always parking on a hill or leaving the engine running. He utilized this method for years.

Ill health finally forced the family to leave. The replacement mis-sionary came and looked under the hood as Herb proudly explained his method of starting the car. The replacement said, "Why, Dr. Jackson, I believe the only problem is this loose cable." He gave the cable a twist and, to Jackson's astonishment, the engine roared to life.

Many of us have a loose cable. We have abandoned prayer and meditation, and as a result, have used up all sorts of needless energy. We are exhausted because we have lost touch with the power source of the universe.

During Superbowl XXXVII, FedEx ran a commercial that spoofed the movie *Castaway,* in which Tom Hanks played a FedEx worker whose company plane went down, stranding him for years on a deserted island. Looking like the bedraggled Hanks in the movie, the FedEx employee in the commercial knocks on the door of a suburban home, package in hand.

When a woman opens the door, the FedEx employee explains that he survived five years on a deserted island, and during that whole time he has kept this package in order to deliver it to her. She gives a simple, "Thank you."

He is curious, however, about what is in the package that he has been protecting all these years and asks her what is in it. She opens it and shows him the contents, saying, "Oh, nothing really . . ." and proceeds to tell him about all the emergency survival gear in it, including a satellite telephone.

Just as the FedEx employee had resources at his disposal of which he was unaware, we have resources at our disposal of which we are aware: prayer and meditation.

You may have noticed that Step Eleven is the longest of the Twelve Steps, not only in words but also in time. We never finish this Step. We do this Step for the rest of our lives because we always are growing spiritually. We always need God's guidance and power.

A five-year-old boy said grace at the dinner table one night. "Dear God," he prayed, "thank you for these pancakes."

When he concluded praying, his parents asked why he had thanked God for pancakes when they were having chicken.

He smiled and said, "I thought I'd see if God was paying attention tonight."

The question is not whether God is paying attention. God is. The question is, are we paying attention to God?

Summary Points to Ponder

- ☙ *A long-time church member confessed, "All my life I have prayed, but I have had very little actual contact with God." Many of us can echo that person's confession. We have prayed consistently and regularly but have had very little actual contact with the Almighty.*

- ☙ *The Eleventh Step is very straightforward. It invites us to build an intimate, spiritual relationship with God.*

- ☙ *How do we make conscious contact with God? First, we have to know it's possible. Second, we may need to correct our faulty image of God.*

- ☙ *Prayer without listening is a one-way street.*

- ☙ *Ever wonder how Jesus could spend the entire night in prayer? He could do it because he spent much of the night listening.*

- ☙ *The Eleventh Step also directs us to pray for the knowledge of God's will "only" for ourselves, and the power to carry it out. That word "only" is very important.*

- ☙ *The knowledge of God's will for our lives is one thing. The power to carry it out is another. Through prayer and meditation we receive this power.*

Personal Exercises

1. Meditate on the following Scriptures over the next few days:
   ✝ a. Psalm 25:4-7
      b. Psalm 40:1-8
      c. Habakkuk 2:1-3
      d. Ephesians 3:14-21
      e. 1 John 1:1-4

2. Set aside three times this week to listen to God. One time focus on an element of God's creation. Another time choose a passage of Scripture to ponder. A third time picture yourself in a favorite place, having a conversation with Jesus.

Group Sharing and Discussion

1. If you could invite three people over for dinner, living or dead, to get to know them better, whom would you invite?

2. What reached out and grabbed you from this chapter?

3. On a scale of one to ten, one being easiest and ten being the hardest, how well do you do when it comes to prayer? Use the same scale for meditation. Explain the reasons for your rankings.

4. If you have had time to do the second "Personal Exercise" above, share your experience with the group. Or share an experience you have had of listening to God.

5. Where could you use a little guidance from God?

Chapter 10

Passing It On

Step 12: Having had a spiritual awakening as the result of these steps, we tried to carry this message to [others], and to practice these principles in all of our affairs.

Leith Anderson, senior pastor of the Woodale Church in Eden Prairie, Minnesota, tells the story of an abbot at a monastery who called a novice into his office and instructed him to give the homily at the next morning's chapel. The request struck the novice with fear. He had never given a homily, let alone to his peers. Public speaking was not his gift or passion.

The next morning, chapel came. He stood before his fellow brothers in the monastery. His hands were trembling. His knees were knocking. His voice was quivering. There was a long pause before he first spoke, and then he asked a question: "Do you know what I'm going to say?"

They had no idea, so all of their heads went back and forth almost in unison, as if it were choreographed. He said, "Neither do I. Let's stand for the benediction."

The next day was almost an exact repeat of the day before. All the brothers sat before him. His hands shook. His knees knocked. His voice trembled. After a long pause he asked, "Do you know what I'm going to say?"

Well, after the previous day's experience, they had a pretty good idea, so they nodded their heads "yes."

"Then there's no need for me to tell you. Let's stand for the benediction."

The abbot was incensed. He brought the young man into his office and said, "If you do that again, you are going to be in solitary confinement, eat bread and water for thirty days, and receive any other punishment I can think of. Tomorrow morning give the homily; do it right."

The third day, chapel attendance hit an all-time high. Everyone was there to see what he would say, and it was almost an exact repeat of the previous days. He stood, trembling, voice quivering, and after a long silence asked, "Do you know what I'm going to say?"

After two days of this, about half of them had a pretty good idea, and they nodded their heads "yes." The other half noticed the switch from day to day, and they weren't sure what to expect, so they shook their heads "no."

The novice observed this and said, "Let those who know tell those who don't. Let us stand for the benediction."[30]

Step Twelve

This story summarizes the final Step. People who know the power of the Twelve Steps tell those who do not. Step Twelve states: *Having had a spiritual awakening as a result of these steps, we tried to carry this message to [others], and to practice these principles in all of our affairs.* In the early days of Alcoholics Anonymous, members went so far as to go to alcoholic wards of local hospitals looking for the worst drunks they could find. They would tell their stories and, if someone showed an interest, they would go on to explain the Twelve Steps.

While that practice may be somewhat extreme, our experience of this vital process of spiritual renewal is too important to keep to ourselves. There are many in need of transformation, living in darkness and bereft of Light, craving healing, hope, love, grace, and peace. The story of God's grace, faithfulness, and love is for everyone. We cannot keep this to ourselves. We need to pass it on.

An obscure, Old Testament story about four lepers comes to mind. Picture the scene. The ancient Arameans invaded Samaria, the northern kingdom of Israel. They surrounded the city and a serious shortage of food ensued.

> Some time later King Ben-hadad of Aram mustered his entire army; he marched against Samaria and laid siege to it. As the siege continued, famine in Samaria became so great that a donkey's head was sold for eighty shekels of silver, and one-fourth of a kab of dove's dung for five shekels of silver. (2 Kings 6:24-25)

A "kab" was an ancient Hebrew unit of measure equal to about two liters. This was a serious situation. People were paying exorbitant prices for donkey heads and liters of dove's dung. (That puts a whole different spin on the question, "What's for dinner?" I won't complain about lima beans ever again!)

Four lepers sat at the city gate of Samaria. They sized up the situation and figured they had a better chance with the Arameans than they did with the Samaritans, so they decided to surrender.

> So they arose at twilight to go to the Aramean camp; but when they came to the edge of the Aramean camp, there was no one there at all. For the Lord had caused the Aramean army to hear the sound of chariots, and of horses, the sound of a great army, so that they said to one another, "The king of Israel has hired the kings of the Hittites and the kings of Egypt to fight against us." So they fled away in the twilight and abandoned their tents, their horses, and their donkeys leaving the camp just as it was, and fled for their lives. When these leprous men had come to the edge of the camp, they went into a tent, ate and drank, carried off silver, gold, and clothing, and went

and hid them. Then they came back, entered another tent, carried off things from it, and went and hid them. (2 Kings 7:5-8)

Those lepers won the lottery. They stumbled upon all sorts of abundance. They went into one tent, stuffed their faces, and found more than they could consume. Not only that, but there was also more to be had in other tents, so they came up with a plan. They decided to find a storage locker and pile up all they had found so they would be set for a long, long time. While stockpiling their bounty, however, they had second thoughts.

> Then they said to one another, "What we are doing is wrong. This is a day of good news; if we are silent and wait until the morning light, we will be found guilty; therefore let us go and tell the king's household." (2 Kings 7:9)

The abundance was so large, the miracle so exciting, the news so wonderful, the lepers had to share it. They also knew they would be in deep weeds if they kept their discovery to themselves. They could predict the questions they would have to answer: "Why didn't you share what you found with us? Why did you keep it to yourselves? We needed what you discovered, and you let us down."

After our experience of the Twelve Steps, why keep it to ourselves? Think about it. When we have good news to share, do we keep it to ourselves? Of course we don't. When we finally get that job, when we get accepted to our favorite college, when we have a great round of golf, when we get engaged, when our children win an award, what do we do? We tell somebody. We tell somebody right away. We may not run all over town, indiscriminately blabbing to everyone we see, but we do tell someone.

In fact, we *need* to share our experience with others. Jesus even encourages us to do it. What Jesus said to the healed demoniac he is saying to us: "Go home to your friends, and tell them how much the Lord has done for you, and what mercy he has shown you" (Mark 5:19). That's exactly what we do in this Twelfth Step: We carry the message of spiritual awakening to others.

Of course, it helps if we are effective carriers. We do not want to come across like telemarketers or door-to-door salespeople or street-corner evangelists. We want to share our news, but how do we do that? What makes for an effective carrier? Four things come to mind.

An Authentic Spiritual Awakening

If we are going to be effective carriers of the message of healing and wholeness, we need to have had an authentic spiritual awakening ourselves. We cannot pass along what we have not experienced.

I love the story behind Elizabeth Barrett Browning's work *Sonnets from the Portuguese*. Many consider these poems to be among the finest love poems ever written. Robert Browning was fond of teasingly calling his wife, Elizabeth, "my little Portuguese" because of her dark complexion. So she titled her love poems to him *Sonnets from the Portuguese*. In the first draft, which she shyly placed in his coat pocket, was the tender line,

> The face of all the world has changed
> since I first heard the footsteps of your soul.

What a beautiful thing to say. It becomes even more beautiful when we can say this about Jesus Christ. For some of us, however, our relationship with Jesus Christ resembles our relationship with George Washington. We know all sorts of things about George. We recognize his picture on the dollar bill. We have read books, heard lectures, and watched movies about him. We know he was the father of our country. We know when he was born, how he chopped down the cherry tree, what he did and said, and how he affected history. There's no doubt in our minds that this leader of the American Revolution really existed. We admire him, respect him, and maybe even revere him. We even celebrate an annual holiday that honors his birthday. We, however, do not know him, at least not personally. We know *about* him, but we do not know him.

Many of us have a similar relationship with Jesus Christ. We know all about him as a historical figure. We know he was a carpenter from Nazareth, that he was born in Bethlehem, that he came as the Son of

God to become the Son of Man, and that he died on the cross for our sins. We believe he existed as much as we believe George Washington existed. We have no doubt about it, and we admire him, respect him, and even celebrate a holiday once a year that honors his birthday. We know all about him, but we don't *know* him. We have not personally encountered the one who can change our souls.

Until we have had an authentic spiritual awakening, we will not be effective carriers of the message. We will not have a personal story to tell. Spiritual awakenings come in all sorts of shapes, colors, and forms. One size does not fit all. Some awakenings are dramatic, some are not. Some come in a twinkling of an eye, some come over time. But they have one thing in common: We are awakened to the presence of a loving, caring, wise, and compassionate God in our lives. As a result of God's presence, our lives have meaning and purpose. We experience a peace and a power unknown to us before our divine encounter. We begin to exhibit the "fruit of the Spirit": "love, joy, peace, patience, kindness, generosity, faithfulness, gentleness, and self-control" (Galatians 5:22-23). We are a new creation.

A Changed Life

A second key to being an effective carrier of the transformational message is a changed life. As the Twelfth Step states, we practice the principles we have learned in all of our affairs. We no longer go through life as we once did. We operate differently. We work the program. We give up, clean up, make up, and keep it up. We walk our talk. We become more trusting of God, ourselves, and others. We become more honest about our strengths and weaknesses. We become willing to make amends and do it regularly. In other words, we are a little like the Apostle Peter.

Scripture shows us a "before and after" Peter. We see a pre-Pentecost Peter and a post-Pentecost Peter. The change is remarkable. The pre-Pentecost Peter was not someone you would go to in a crunch. In his early years, whenever he opened his mouth, it was to change feet. Peter was the one who often had egg on his face. Maybe that is why so many claim Peter as their favorite disciple, because he was so human, so much like us.

But after Pentecost, after the Holy Spirit came upon him, something happened to Peter. When Peter got up to preach on the day of Pentecost, some might have cringed. They might have thought, "Oh, no, what's he going to say now? He's had so many embarrassing moments; he's made so many blunders." Peter, however, said exactly what was needed, and three thousand people gave all they knew of themselves to all they knew of Jesus Christ that morning. All of a sudden, we see the Peter Jesus predicted when Jesus nicknamed him "The Rock."

And if we did not know any better, we would find it hard to believe that the Peter described in the Book of Acts is the same Peter we got to know in the Gospels. There is such a difference in the man. In Acts 3 Peter healed a crippled beggar. Later he was beaten and flogged and imprisoned, but he kept on preaching the gospel—no more stealing away in the dark, as he did the night of Jesus's arrest. Then in Acts 9 he raised a woman from the dead. Now, that's a major healing! A head cold is one thing, a little blindness is another, but Peter raised Dorcas from the dead!

After working the Twelve Steps, we, too, become Mr. and Ms. "Before and After." We have changed . . . and we are changing. We are slowly and steadily growing into the image of Christ. We are not yet what we are going to be, but we are no longer who we once were. As a result, others notice the difference, and they want to know what's happening. If we make a relational, emotional, or behavioral change, people are curious. If we are not as negative anymore, sooner or later someone will ask, "I've noticed that you seem more positive than you used to be. How come?" And then we tell them. We tell them how God has restored us to sanity. We tell them what God has been doing in our lives and how the Twelve Steps have helped us.

A changed life is one of the most effective witnesses to the work of Jesus Christ in the world. The proof is in the pudding. Healthier relationships, a vibrant authenticity, a clear conscience, and a newfound sense of the presence of God all open the door for us. When people see the difference in us, they often invite us in to tell our story.

A Compassionate Heart

The third key to being an effective carrier is compassion. Being a relatively new grandfather, I resonate with a grandfather who, on Thanksgiving Day, explained to his little grandson the custom of breaking the turkey wishbone. Eager to have his wish come true, the boy was crushed when his grandfather got the largest portion of bone. "That's all right, my boy," said his grandfather with a smile. "I made a wish, and my wish was that you would get your wish."

To want what is best for others is at the center of this Twelfth Step, and it is a key to being an effective carrier. Contrast this sort of carrier with another sort of carrier. I love the title of the book *The Church with Something to Offend Almost Everyone.* I loved the book even more, and one section particularly struck me. The author of the book and pastor of the Broadway Baptist Church, Paul Smith, relates what being a carrier meant to him:

> In the church of my youth I was basically taught that one of the major jobs of Christians was to shove people up against the wall and frisk them for bad doctrine. The thrill of heresy hunting, sect slashing, Catholic castigating, and liberal lashing was one of the great blessings of being a Christian. The harm of such religious abuse and hate tactics is incalculable and it took me well into my twenties to get out of that unchristian mindset.[31]

Unfortunately, some still think that's what it means to be a carrier: "If I'm going to be effective, I'll have to be pushy. I'll have to be argumentative. I'll have to be judgmental and narrow." Who wants to be like that? I don't. You don't . . . well, most of you don't! But that's not what it takes to be effective. The requirement of being an effective carrier is to have a heart, to want the best for other people. Effective carriers communicate their interest. They listen. They sympathize. They make others feel important.

The majority of us can look back on our lives and identify people who genuinely cared about us and wanted what was best for us. They were able to say things to us others could not because they had earned the right to be heard. We trusted them. We loved them, and they loved us. We can also identify people who did not care about us. They had a product to sell or a viewpoint to get across, and we did not buy it. They only cared about the sale, not us.

A wise friend of mine said that people want three questions answered about their pastor: "Does my pastor love me? Does my pastor still love me? Will my pastor continue to love me?" He said, "If a congregation answers 'yes' to all three questions, the pastor will have an effective ministry."

When we carry the message to others, they share the same questions: "Do you love me? Do you still love me? Will you continue to love me even though I do not buy into the Twelve Steps?" If our answer is "yes," we will be effective carriers.

A Story to Tell, Not a Sermon to Preach

After twenty-five years of being a pastor, I know when I'm losing people's interest during a sermon. The noise level in the congregation rises, ever so slightly. There are more coughs and more clearing of throats. More people check their watches. When I shift gears during a message, however, and move from theology to a personal story, that all changes. When I share the raw material from my life, eyes move front and center, heads nod in identification, and you can hear a pin drop. Why? Because story telling is more effective than preaching or teaching. This is the fourth key to being an effective carrier.

The entire world loves a good story, whether it's a nursery rhyme about Humpty Dumpty, a fairy tale about a wicked witch, a fable from Aesop, a story about a mermaid with dreams of being human, or an allegory about a hobbit on his way to Mt. Doom. And Jesus knew that. It's no accident that he chose story form for over one-third of his recorded teachings. He often launched into a story, using phrases such as, "A sower went to sow seed . . ." or "There was a rich man who had a manager . . ." or "Someone gave a great dinner and invited many . . ." or "There was a man who had two sons . . .", and immediately he had his audience's attention.

John Alexander, a teacher of philosophy and a columnist for *The Other Side* magazine, reminds us,

When God came to be among us he didn't come as a mathematician or a scientist. He came as a storyteller. Not as Newton and Einstein rolled into one but as Sophocles-Dante. And he told stories people could live. At bottom, the Judeo-Christian tradition isn't a list of rules or a set of scientific theories; it's a big, long story. The hundreds of pages of story and poetry in the Bible are not an accident but the very medium through which God speaks.[32]

Somewhere along the way, we got it all wrong. We thought to be effective carriers, we needed to know the Bible backward and forward. We needed to know the difference between Docetism and Gnosticism. We needed to know the answer to questions such as, "Did Adam and Eve have navels?" and "What exactly is an ephod?" We thought to be effective carriers, we needed to win every argument, answer every objection, and field every question. But we knew we could not do that, so we took a pass. We decided that we could never be an effective carrier.

We were wrong. What makes for an effective carrier is someone with a personal story to tell of God's love, grace, forgiveness, and healing, and we *can* tell that story. We can tell someone the difference Jesus Christ is making in our lives. People may argue with our politics or our theology, but not our story. We are the authority when it comes to our own story. It's ours to tell and ours alone. It's also more powerful than we can ever imagine.

In the year he was elected president, Jimmy Carter was one of three men invited to speak to the seventeen thousand delegates at the Southern Baptist Convention. Each had a five-minute time limit. The first of the three presenters was the eloquent evangelist Billy Graham. The speaker following Graham was a truck driver. Carter admitted he was glad to be following the truck driver, and not Graham. He said, "At least I'll sound good in comparison."

The truck driver shared with Carter how he had never given a speech in his life. Drenched with sweat, he nervously confessed, "I don't think I can live through it. I just can't do it." Carter did all he could to keep the truck driver from fleeing the scene.

After Billy Graham gave his powerful talk, the truck driver rose to speak and stood silently before the audience. He stood silently for a long time. Taking a glass of water that someone handed to him, he finally mumbled into the microphone, "I was always drunk, and didn't have any friends. The only people I knew were men like me who hung around the bars in the town where I lived." He proceeded to tell his story about the difference Christ had made, and was making, in his life.

Carter said, "The truck driver's speech, of course, was the highlight of the convention. I don't believe anyone who was there will ever forget that five-minute fumbling statement—or remember what I or even Billy Graham had to say."[33]

Everyone loves a good story . . . including ours.

Summary Points to Ponder

◉ *There are many in need of transformation, living in darkness and bereft of Light, craving healing, hope, love, grace, and peace. The story of God's grace, faithfulness, and love is for everyone. We cannot keep this to ourselves. We need to pass it on.*

◉ *People who know the power of the Twelve Steps tell those who do not.*

◉ *If we are going to be effective carriers of the message of healing and wholeness, we need to have had an authentic spiritual awakening ourselves. We cannot pass along what we have not experienced.*

◉ *A changed life is one of the most effective witnesses to the work of Jesus Christ in the world. When people see the difference in us, they often invite us in to tell our story.*

◉ *When we carry the message to others, they want to know, "Do you love me? Do you still love me? Will you continue to love me even though I do not buy into the Twelve Steps?" If our answer is "yes," we will be effective carriers.*

◉ *Everyone loves a good story . . . including ours.*

Personal Exercises

1. Reflect and meditate on the following Scriptures:
    a. Isaiah 61:1-4
    b. Mark 5:18-20
    c. Psalm 96:1-4
    d. Acts 1:8
    e. Philippians 3:12-14

2. Write your story of God's transforming power in your life. See if you can get it down to one page. Be ready to share it if someone asks you about the change they see in you.

For Group Sharing and Discussion

1. Who was one of the first effective carriers of God's love, grace, and forgiveness to you? Who was an ineffective carrier?

2. What is holding you back from being an effective carrier?
    a. Have not had an authentic spiritual awakening.
    b. I do not want to appear pushy or obnoxious.
    c. I do not think my story is very interesting.
    d. What's worked for me might not work for someone else.
    e. I want to make sure the changes stick before talking about them.
    f. Nothing. I'm ready to get the word out.
    g. Other.

3. What grabbed you from this chapter?

4. What was a high point in this Twelve Step process for you? A low point?

5. What have you appreciated about the group?

Endnotes

Section One: The Give Up Steps

Chapter One: The Great Admission

1. Philip Yancey, *What's So Amazing About Grace?*, 275-76.
2. As quoted by Helen Smith Shoemaker, *I Stand by the Door*, 192.
3. Patricia Campbell-Schmitt sermon, "Wanted: A God Who Can Help," September 27, 1992.
4. Keith Miller, *Sin: Overcoming the Ultimate Deadly Addiction*, 46.

Chapter Two: "Help, I Need Somebody"

5. *Alcoholics Anonymous*, 44-45.
6. Dick B., *Turning Point*, 158.
7. James W. Cox, *The Twentieth Century Pulpit*, 50.
8. Richard J. Foster, *Prayer: Finding the Heart's True Home*, 179.

Chapter Three: The Big Decision

9. *Finding Nemo* (Disney/Pixar), 2003.
10. Dick B., *Turning Point*, 178.
11. *Alcoholics Anonymous*, 61.
12. Laura Hillenbrand, *Seabiscuit: An American Legend*, 27.

13. As quoted by John Ortberg, *If You Want to Walk on Water You've Got to Get Out of the Boat*, 24.

Section Two: The Clean Up Steps
Chapter Four: Making a List and Checking It Twice
14. *Alcoholics Anonymous*, 68-69.
15. Ibid., 64.
16. As cited by Dick B., *Turning Point*, 256.

Chapter Five: Coming Clean
17. John F. Westfall, *Coloring Outside the Lines*, 24-25.
18. John Bunyan, *The Pilgrim's Progress*, 39.
19. Charles R. Swindoll, *The Quest for Character*, 110.
20. As quoted in *Martin Luther Werke and Kritische Gesammtausgabe* (Weimer: Herman Bohler, 1888), 546.
21. Mary Chambers, *The Best Cartoons from Leadership Journal*, Volume 1. Used by permission of Mary Chambers.
22. Kenneth Quick, "Confidentiality: 'Will You Tell' Overture," *Leadership Journal*, Summer 1991, 102.

Chapter Six: Get Ready, Get Set, Go
23. Laura Beth Jones, *Jesus in Blue Jeans: A Practical Guide to Everyday Spirituality*, 252-53.
24. *Alcoholics Anonymous*, 76

Section Four: The Keep It Up Steps
Chapter Eight: Ongoing Reflection and Repentance
25. *The Preacher's Illustration Service* (Ventnor, N.J.: Preacher's Illustration Service, 2000), Vol. 12, No. 2, 7.

Chapter Nine: Staying in Touch with God
26. Marshall Ziemann sermon, "Making Conscious Contact with God," August 8, 1993.
27. "In the Garden," text by C. Austin Miles, 1913.
28. David R. Hosick sermon, "Power to Do God's Will," February 19, 1995.
29. Norman Vincent Peale, "When You Pray—Really Pray," *Plus: The Magazine of Positive Thinking*, January/February 1996, 8.

Chapter Ten: Passing It On
30. Leith Anderson, "Making More Disciples," *Preaching Today*, 165.
31. Paul Smith, *The Church with Something to Offend Almost Everyone*, 99.
32. John F. Alexander, *The Secular Squeeze*, 114.
33. Jimmy Carter, *Sources of Strength*, 72.

Bibliography

Alcoholics Anonymous (Third Edition), New York: Alcoholics Anonymous World Services, 1976.

Alexander, John, *The Secular Squeeze*, Downers Grove, Ill.: Intervarsity Press, 1993.

Anderson, Leith, "Making More Disciples," *Preaching Today*, Carol Stream, Ill.: Christianity Today, Sermon 165.

B., Dick, *Turning Point: A History of Early A.A.'s Spiritual Roots and Successes*, Kihei, Hawaii: Paradise Research Publications, 1997.

Bunyan, John, *The Pilgrim's Progress*, London: J.M. Dent & Sons, 1954.

Carter, Jimmy, *Sources of Strength*, New York: Time Books, 1997.

Cox, James W., *The Twentieth Century Pulpit*, Nashville: Abingdon, 1978.

Foster, Richard J., *Prayer: Finding the Heart's True Home*, San Francisco: Harper, 1992.

Hillenbrand, Laura, *Seabiscuit: An American Legend*, New York: Random House, 2001.

Jones, Laura Beth, *Jesus in Blue Jeans: A Practical Guide to Everyday Spirituality*, New York: Hyperion, 1997.

Miller, J. Keith, *Sin: Overcoming the Ultimate Deadly Addiction*, San Francisco: Harper & Row, 1987.

Ortberg, John, *If You Want to Walk on Water You've Got to Get Out of the Boat*, Grand Rapids, Mich.: Zondervan, 2001.

Peale, Norman Vincent, "When You Pray—Really Pray," *Plus: The Magazine of Positive Thinking*, New York: The Peale Center, January/February, 1996.

Quick, Kenneth, "Confidentiality: 'Will You Tell' Overture," *Leadership Journal*, Carol Stream, Ill.: Christianity Today, Summer 1991.

Shoemaker, Helen Smith, *I Stand by the Door*, Waco, Tex.: Word Books, 1967.

Smith, Paul, *The Church with Something to Offend Almost Everyone*, Kansas City, Mo.: Paul Smith, 1992.

Sose, Bonnie, *Talk to Me: 1777 Intimate Questions, Share Your Heart with a Loved One*, Winter Park, Fla.: Character Builders, 1991.

Swindoll, Charles, *The Quest for Character*, Portland: Multnomah Press, 1987.

Westfall, John F., *Coloring Outside the Lines*, San Francisco: Harper Collins, 1991.

Yancey, Philip, *What's So Amazing About Grace?* Grand Rapids, Mich.: Zondervan, 1997.